THE LANGUAGE OF TEACHING

Meaning in Classroom Interaction

Also by A. D. Edwards:

Language in Culture and Class
The Sociology of Language and Education

THE LANGUAGE OF TEACHING

Meaning in Classroom Interaction

A. D. Edwards and V. J. Furlong

HEINEMANN · LONDON

Heinemann Educational Books Ltd

LONDON EDINBURGH MELBOURNE AUCKLAND TORONTO
HONG KONG SINGAPORE KUALA LUMPUR NEW DELHI
NAIROBI JOHANNESBURG LUSAKA IBADAN
KINGSTON

Cased edition ISBN 0 435 80294 1
Paper edition ISBN 0 435 80295 X
© A. D. Edwards and V. J. Furlong 1978
First published 1978

Published by Heinemann Educational Books Ltd
48 Charles Street, London W1X 8AH
Typesetting by George Over Ltd, Rugby and London
Printed in Great Britain by Richard Clay (The Chaucer Press) Ltd,
Bungay, Suffolk

Contents

Chapter 1

Introduction: Talking About Teaching

Throughout most of the history of educational research, it has been common practice to 'measure the results of teaching while neglecting teaching itself'.(1) Those researchers who did enter the classroom usually retreated from the bewildering complexity of classroom life into the apparent safety of 'scientific' methods of observing it. Classrooms are extraordinarily busy places, and with so much to observe it was undoubtedly tempting for researchers to use a fine sieve in which to catch only those events they felt to be really significant. But teachers looking for practical guidance were likely to find such studies too arid and too coolly rational. Even if researchers could cope with the complexities of classroom interaction by concentrating on 'essentials', teachers clearly cannot do so. They are therefore likely to be impatient with cleaned-up, tidy versions of what they know to be a very untidy reality. If they often seem indifferent or hostile to educational research, it is partly because so much of it appears remote from the problems which they encounter daily. Their indifference has been sympathetically explained by Philip Jackson as one outcome of the enormous amount of ambiguity, unpredictability and occasional chaos created each hour by twenty-five or thirty not-so-willing learners. Jackson found in teachers' accounts of their daily work an uncomplicated view of causality, an intuitive rather than a rational approach to classroom events, an unwillingness to consider alternative teaching practices, and a limited technical vocabulary. This summary was not intended as a scathing indictment of unprofessional behaviour, but as the description of a realistic adjustment to a situation so complex and fluid that a more thoroughly planned and rational approach would leave teachers unable to cope at all. Teaching depended on endless improvisation, a constant readiness to adapt any plans that had been made to the circumstances of the moment.(2)

What we have outlined here is a large and persistent difference in perspective between participant and observer. Facing the rapidly changing details of classroom life, teachers rarely have either the time or the detachment to contemplate the forms it takes. If no observer can ever know their situation as they know it, his distance from the action may make it possible to suggest ways of reflecting on their activities and so 'discovering their own situation'.(3) But how can it be argued that teachers need to discover a situation which they cope with every working day? Is there not a brazen arrogance in such a claim to bring 'news'—to reveal that 'real' situation to which the participants themselves are frequently blind?

The justification for this claim does *not* come from assuming some ultimate reality which only the expert social scientist is equipped to penetrate. It arises from the extreme difficulty of seeing what is familiar and recurrent. If the immediacy and pace of classroom events make it essential for teachers to make most of their work a matter of routine, then what is routine may have to be 'forced out of its usual semi-consciousness' if it is to be reflected upon at all.(4) Introducing the first (and still the most comprehensive and perceptive) sociology of teaching nearly fifty years ago, Willard Waller showed what insights into the 'social realities of school life' could be obtained from the 'systematic wondering . . . of a reasonably acute observer'. Any merit to be found in his account was identified as being 'the merit of the commonplace'.(5) In the present state of the discipline, he argued, no sociologist could hope to get very far ahead of commonsense and would be lucky to avoid falling far behind it. There was therefore a high risk of saying things about classrooms which had not been said before because no-one had ever thought them worth saying; they were simply part of what everyone knew. Now their capacity to state the obvious has been an endemic criticism of social scientists, and a common defence against the resulting risk of being declared redundant has been to talk about familiar things in ways that suddenly make them appear strange and mysterious. This may bring fresh insights. It may also be just a different way of saying what everyone knows, a literal translation into another 'language' which baffles the reader without adding anything to his understanding. A 'smoke-screen of jargon' then hides the platitudes, because no-one is sure how much or how little is being said.(6) Waller explicitly renounced any such smoke-screen. He chose to write his book in a style 'as non-technical as it was possible to be without the loss of essential meanings'. We have tried hard to do this ourselves. But much more is involved in the task than an avoidance of jargon. Waller was anxious to present his material 'in the idiom with which it naturally consorts in the folk-talk of teachers' — that is, to talk about teaching as teachers talk about it themselves. But as his earlier comment suggests, there may be times when this practice brings a loss of 'essential meanings'. However alert the social scientist is to the danger of artificially (and defensively) sharpening the boundaries between 'scientific' and 'everyday' language, he may still feel that 'folk-talk' is not always adequate for making sense of folk-ways because such talk reinforces that very sense of the inevitability of familiar things which he is seeking to disturb. If there is always the likelihood of saying what is obvious, there is also the possibility of saying some things which are not normally seen because they *are* so obvious. It is extremely difficult to regard the commonplace with enough detachment to avoid an instant feeling of '*This* is it, *this* is what is going on' and to see through the surface of obstinately familiar scenes. The familiarity of classrooms is especially obstinate. We have all spent so much time in them, and teachers and pupils produce and cope with their routines every working day. This very familiarity makes it hard to see what is happening, and to make sense of it, in other than conventional ways. That basic difference in perspective between teacher and observer therefore contains some potential advantages.

In a book explicitly intended to help teachers to be more reflective about conventional practices, Stubbs comments on their lack of 'an adequate descriptive language for talking about their own professional behaviour'.(7) His recommended alternative to 'mere surface description' is description *within* some theoretical framework for interpreting what is being described, and he sees the provision of such a framework as the best service that researchers can do for teachers. It might be described as a sequential collaboration. The analytical tools are designed, sharpened in use, and then handed over to teachers for them to use in the classrooms they know best. This is an approach with which we feel a great deal of sympathy, and we return to it in our final chapter when we reflect on the tools which we developed ourselves. While quite properly blurring the distinction between 'expert' and teacher, it still offers a justification for classroom research. Teachers may be *too* familiar with their situation to see some of its critical features, and too preoccupied with daily routines (and emergencies) to be able to step back and reflect on what is going on. The researcher has time for reflection, and perhaps the detachment to ask questions about what is normally taken for granted. He may therefore be able to present the ordinary in a somewhat different light.(8)

This advocacy of a *different* perspective must not be taken as implying that the researcher is somehow equipped to see what is really going on. The alternative to 'mere surface description' is *not* the revelation of what unquestionably lies beneath the surface. Depending on his theoretical vantage-point, the researcher will see things differently not only from the teacher but from other researchers too. Stubb's separation of description from the theory which makes sense of it implies misleadingly that 'mere' description is possible. It is not. Teachers' own descriptions of their professional behaviour rest on explicit or implicit theories of teaching. In so far as these descriptions *are* inadequate, it may be because the theories simply confirm current practice. Supposedly objective records of class-room behaviour made by specially trained observers are full of theoretical assumptions, even when they are presented as the neutral fact-finding which *precedes* analysis. As we argue in Chapter 3, the issue is not theory or no theory, but what sort of theory? So while our introductory argument proceeded as though there was some single researcher's perspective to be contrasted with the participants' view of classroom events, much of our book is concerned with the variety of available perspectives. What research provides is a diversity of ways of talking about teaching, each of which reflects the preoccupations of the researcher and captures different aspects of classroom life.

Does this mean, then, that social scientists are forever working out their preconceptions, and so generating an indefinite series of different accounts, each true to itself but none more valid than the others? Much of the next two chapters might suggest that we believe this to be the case. In Chapter 2, we review what 'research has shown' about the distinctive characteristics of classroom talk, and about the shaping of meaning to which these contribute. We do so in a deliberately eclectic way, making use of evidence of very different kinds. In the next chapter, we consider how this evidence was obtained, emphasizing the different pictures of classroom life produced from different perspectives. But a proper appreciation of the many-sidedness of truth does not necessarily imply parity of esteem for all versions. Researchers would find it hard to keep going if they did not believe, at least some of the time, that their approach had something special to offer — that alternatives were not only different but in some sense worse. The analysis presented in Chapter 3 is therefore directed, quite partially, towards the approach which we adopted ourselves.

Some of the alternatives have seemed to work by greatly simplifying the phenomena, even treating classrooms as places where teachers can convert their wants into reality by systematically controlling their own behaviour.(9) This makes teaching look too easy. It also assumes that classrooms are places where 'teachers normally tell pupils what to do, how to do it, when to start, when to stop, and how well they did whatever they did'.(10) In so far as classrooms *are* like this, it could be argued that they have got the research methods they deserve. Certainly, the main facts about them are much easier to establish than is the case with the more fragmented interaction characteristic of informal classrooms, because most observation schedules have to be packed away when anything markedly different from conventional class teaching is taking place. As we commented at the start of this chapter, most classroom researchers have coped with the stream of verbal behaviour by burying what is said in some category-system. This systematic approach has its place — for example, in extensive surveys of the strategies used in teaching particular school subjects — but it does little to diminish our 'spectacular ignorance' of the actual language of the classroom.(11) About the kinds of talk generated by resource-based learning, almost nothing is known at all.(12) It has also been a frequent criticism of mainstream research that its reports were so abstracted from the life of the classroom that those hankering for a sense of reality were driven either to fiction or to the vivid insiders' reports of teachers like John Holt, Edward Blishen, or Jonathan Kozol. We share with Waller a belief in the value of *intensive* research, because it makes possible so much detail that 'characters do not lose the qualities of persons, nor situations their intrinsic human reality'. In our own account, we have tried to convey the 'human reality' of the classrooms we observed, and to confront at least some of the neglected complexities of the interaction.

The next two chapters report the groundwork for our research by looking at what is known about the shaping of meaning in classroom interaction, and then at some of the perspectives from which these 'facts' were produced. This groundwork brought a considerable paralysis of the empirical nerve. Classroom talk often seemed so complex that we wondered how it was possible to make sense of it at all, and envied the confidence of some other researchers that they could capture what really occurred. The predominantly critical tone of Chapter 3 reflects a long preoccupation with problems.(13) The end of that chapter reports our eventual abandonment of the relatively comfortable role of critical spectator for the trials of actually playing the game.

We went into that game with only a general idea of what we wanted to look for, which was to see how teachers and pupils talked into existence the relationships and meanings which would dominate their work together. But however general that interest may seem, it determined our choice of a school in which to work. Most of the approaches discussed in Chapter 3 share a wariness of unconventional classrooms because the interaction may lack an identifiable structure with which the researcher can get to grips. Yet that familiarity of traditional classrooms to which we referred earlier often leads researchers themselves to trade heavily on their own (and their readers') knowledge of what such classrooms are like without reflecting on *how*, and how much, they do so. We wanted to find a less familiar setting, one which would force us to work harder if we wanted to follow what was going on. We were also interested in what such classrooms were like. What did teachers do instead of 'telling' in contexts where self-imposed restrictions on class teaching were tight?

We chose to work in the Abraham Moss Centre because it contains the most overtly innovative of Manchester's comprehensive schools. Its main features are described in Chapter 4, which sets the scene for a detailed account of the one part of its work which we observed closely — the teaching of Humanities in the Lower School. We are very indebted to the Centre's Principal, Mr Ron Mitson, and to the Head of Lower School, Miss Pat Logan, for their ready agreement to our working there. Their co-operation went beyond acquiescence to actively removing many of those tangible and intangible barriers which classroom researchers so often face. Inevitably, much of the teaching material we saw being used, and many of the ideas underlying it, had been developed by previous members of the Humanities team. We are therefore grateful to David Parden (Consultant for Humanities at the Centre), Janet Harris, Judy Loeb, and David Watchorn, for filling in the necessary background, and enabling us to see the teaching we actually observed in a longer perspective.(14) Our heaviest debt is obviously to the five teachers — Liz Burr, Alan Clegg, Rod Hill, Liz Isaac, and Rob Isaac — who allowed us to watch them at work, discussed our interpretations of what they were doing without any sign of defensiveness, and never treated us as intruders. Our respect for their work should be apparent in the chapters which follow.

Before we began work at the school, we circulated a letter to those teachers with whom we would be directly involved, and to other members of staff who might be interested in (or suspicious of) what we were up to. Most of this letter is quoted in Chapter 4, because it sets out what we thought we were doing when the research began. Of course, we came out with something rather different. As we argue later, it is always tempting to find convenient examples for preconceived ideas. But the contrasting image of the open-minded researcher building his theory entirely from his observations seems to us quite unrealistic. While we are aware of many changes in our thinking during the course of the research, there is no way in which we can separate those parts which are grounded in an intensive study of the lesson transcripts from those which simply illustrate what we expected to find. Our analysis, constructed and preconstructed, is reported in Chapters 5—7.

Perhaps the greatest change in our ideas during the two years was a change in objective. At the beginning, our intentions could be described as mainly theoretical. We hoped to contribute to the development of a 'language' for talking about teaching which could cope with the basic features of classroom talk, and which avoided any separation of the management of the interaction from the management of meanings. If things went well, such a contribution would be reported in the normal academic channels. As the work proceeded, however, our concern with making a contribution to theory merged with increasingly practical intentions. The first of these we have mentioned already. We wanted to describe a kind of teaching of which very little is known. Although mixed-ability classes are now common in secondary schools, teaching which takes account of this diversity is not. Recipes prescribing how it ought to be done are far more readily available than detailed descriptions of how it *is* done. We also wanted to describe such teaching in the kind of inner-city context stereotypically associated with chaos. We do not suggest that the teachers we observed have solved all their instructional and disciplinary problems, and they would certainly not claim this themselves. But in most of the lessons we recorded, we were impressed by an atmosphere which was both relaxed and workmanlike. In a difficult area, these teachers seemed largely to avoid the endless confrontations with pupils which are supposedly so prevalent, and to be able to get down to 'work'.

As we observed and analysed the teaching, we came to feel that there was a useful reporting job to be done. But even at their most practical, our ambitions extended beyond descriptive journalism. We also hoped to develop ways of thinking about classroom interaction which could be applied, in suitably modified form, to other contexts. The *results* of such a limited study as ours are obviously not open to generalization. But the *kind* of analysis we present might well have a general value. This possibility has influenced the style in which the book is written, and in the direction taken by Waller. It may well be possible to write for two audiences, social scientists and teachers, who have different concerns and different working vocabularies. But we doubt whether these two audiences can be given equal priority. Where we felt the need to choose between them, we have chosen to write for teachers. There are two reasons for this. Even in the period since we began work late in 1975, a great deal of intensive classroom research has been published in readily accessible form.(15) Much of it, however, has been so preoccupied with theoretical problems as to be largely incomprehensible to those without a considerable background in social science, and to be hard going even for social scientists if they lacked the particular vocabulary in which it was written. When badly needed alternatives to systematic research are still in the exploratory stage, it is certainly important that specialists should clear some of the ground for one another. But like the poet's duty to write for other men as well as for other poets, some classroom researchers should surely be writing for classroom teachers. A few, like Douglas Barnes, have consistently suceeded in doing so. A few have tried so hard that they have thrown out the baby with the academic bath-water. We have tried to avoid merely simplifying, referring at the end of each chapter not only to other relevant classroom studies but also to more general theories which influenced our approach. In the text itself, however, the theory is largely implicit. The only prolonged exceptions to the theoretical introspection which is now so fashionable will be found in Chapters 3 and 8.

The second reason why we have tried to write for teachers returns this Introduction to the point from which it began. Classrooms are much too complex for researchers to be able to tell teachers 'how to do it'. What they can do, perhaps, is to suggest some ways of making sense of classroom interaction, and some questions about the forms it takes. In the division of labour between them, the researcher has a degree of detachment in his role as observer, and some time to reflect on what he sees. But he can never know the situation as the teacher knows it, and there will be very few classrooms that he can know at all. Like David Hargreaves and his colleagues, we have sought 'a more adequate conceptual framework' for considering classroom talk, but we have given priority to what they state as their second and equal aim — to elucidate for teachers 'what (in one sense) they already know, and thereby lay some foundation for the development of practical insights into their everyday problems'.(16)

Chapter 1: Notes and References

(Full details are given in the Bibliography.)

1   Skinner (1968), *The Technology of Teaching*, p. 94. Though Skinner's criticism was directed at educational psychologists, sociologists were no less prone to relate educational input to educational output without paying serious attention to the process of 'manufacture'. This neglect is discussed in Walker (1972), 'The Sociology of Education and Life in School Classrooms', *Int. Rev. Educ.* 18.
2   Jackson (1968), *Life in Classrooms*, pp. 143–150.
3   Walker and Adelman (1975b), *A Guide to Classroom Observation*, p. 6. The authors' declared intention is to help teachers 'to become their own researchers and evaluators'.
4   Stebbins (1975), *Teachers and Meanings*, p. 125.

5   Waller (1965), *The Sociology of Teaching*, preface and p. 3. This book was first published in 1932.

6   For a fervent but undiscriminating onslaught on jargon, see Andreski (1974), *Social Science as Sorcery*, Chapter 6.

7   Stubbs (1976), *Language, Schools and Classrooms*, p. 71.

8   The essential difference in perspective is described by Walker and Adelman, op. cit., p. 25, in a form close to the argument which we develop in our final chapter. Coping with the immediacy of classroom events, the teacher is likely to see a fluid, transient, and fragile situation, where the observer may see 'a relatively stable, concrete, socially structured series of events'.

9   For a striking example of such confidence, see Meacham and Wiesen (1973), *Changing Classroom Behaviour: A Manual for Precision Teaching*.

10   Flanders (1970), *Analysing Teacher Behaviour*, p. 14.

11   This point is elaborated in Edwards (1976), *Language in Culture and Class*, chapter 5.

12   The neglect can persist even when entire curriculum packages are built on learning of this kind. A recent attempt to remedy it in relation to Nuffield Science is described in Eggleston *et al.* (1976), *The Processes and Products of Science Teaching*. In this research, a specially devised observation schedule made it possible to 'cover' almost 100 classrooms.

13   Our preoccupation with difficulties is apparent in Furlong and Edwards (1977), 'Language in Classroom Interaction: Theory and Data', *Educ. Research* 14.

14   This longer perspective should include two teachers, John Blatchford and Judy Dyson, who have now left the Centre.

15   E.g. Chanan and Delamont (1975), *Frontiers of Classroom Research;* Hammersley and Woods (1976), *The Process of Schooling*; Stubbs and Delamont (1976), *Explorations in Classroom Observations*; Woods and Hammersley (1977), *School Experience*.

16   The preface to Hargreaves *et al.* (1975), *Deviance in Classrooms*.

Chapter 2

Characteristics of Classroom Talk

Introduction

The most obvious characteristic of classroom talk is that there is so much of it. Whatever else he does, the teacher will be talking for most of his working day. If most of this talking is done in small groups and with individual children, then he may escape that vocal fate predicted by Waller — the 'didactic voice' which has been drained of emotion and enthusiasm by the endless repetition of facts. But in most classrooms, certainly in secondary schools, there is likely to be a predominance of talk as a public performance. Even in the absence of any hard evidence about what has been learned, the articulate teacher is likely to be judged effective and articulate pupils are more likely to have their ability recognized.

Classrooms as we know them are such wordy places that we may assume, like the Bullock Committee, that a lesson 'naturally' involves the verbal exposition of facts and skills — that it is 'a verbal encounter through which the teacher draws information from the class, elaborates and generalizes it, and produces a synthesis'.(1) This assumption illustrates the general difficulty of observing a setting so familiar that its distinctive features are not easily questioned or even noticed. Yet there are cultures where instruction depends more on watching, imitation, and silent practice than on an endless stream of words. There are cross-cultural classrooms where children's experience in their home world leads them to reject teachers' demands that they demonstrate verbally and in public a competence only recently acquired, and to resist expectations that they should either speak or be silent as the teacher requires.(2) Even in our own culture, classroom research is sometimes criticized for over-emphasizing verbal interaction to an extent unsuited to the more visual and physically active forms of learning encouraged in many primary schools. There are certainly classrooms where the talk is too dispersed and private to be representatively recorded from some central point, and where so much is happening alongside the talk that only a visual record could begin to capture the complexity of events. Such classrooms are found in secondary schools too. But except by default, where order has broken down, they remain rare. Verbal encounters are still the main means of transmitting knowledge, and they are encounters of a very distinctive kind. For older children especially, the main characteristics of classroom talk are not only that there is so much of it, but that so much of what is said is both public and highly centralized. The following example is commonplace, any stylistic variations staying close to the theme:(3)

2.1   T: OK, we'll start in a minute. We'll just wait till everybody's quiet. What I want to do is run through it with everybody to make sure that people understand what the two stories . . . *Do you mind*. What was I just saying, John?
       P: ((Mutters inaudibly.))
       T: Right, you were busy talking were you. Why? ((Silence.)) We've not got time to waste, John. We need to do this so *everybody* knows what they're doing. So don't waste any more time, please.

The theme is, simply, 'everybody listen'. For much of the time in classrooms, there is a *single* verbal encounter in which whatever is being said demands the attention of all.

In the first part of this chapter, we argue that such centralized communication is both an extraordinary fact and a remarkable achievement. We also see it as imposing a persistently heavy strain on the teacher, who has to hold things together in this way. For many teachers, it is here that their main problems lie. It is impossible, however, to separate the organization of classroom talk from the management of classroom meanings. If we seem initially to be doing so, it is only for descriptive convenience. We will look first at what makes classrooms so distinctive as settings for talk, and at how orderly interaction is achieved and maintained. But the emphasis throughout the chapter will be on the shaping of meaning in a context 'set up primarily for the control of knowledge by the patterning of communication'.(4)

1 Centralized Communication

Classrooms are crowded places. Yet despite the presence of thirty or so potential communicators, what has been called a 'central communication system' is frequent and often prolonged. What this means is that everybody else listens (or gives the appearance of listening) to a single speaker, and that any 'small enclaves of private interaction . . . are typically transitory'.(5) In the research which this statement refers to, a central system contained *all* the talk taking place for three-quarters of the lesson time recorded. When private enclaves did appear, those involved were usually located at the back or along the sides of the room, and so were outside a 'central communication zone' which extended in a broad V from the teacher's desk. Though their activities might be tolerated for a time, they were quickly terminated if they became too obtrusive. The teacher was normally central to the interaction, both physically and communicatively. Indeed, such importance seemed to be attached to his front-of-stage location that any straying from it, except to show the disciplinary flag, was associated with a sudden upsurge of private conversation.

Certainly the pervasiveness of this centralized communication should not be exaggerated. A great deal of unofficial talk both surrounds and intrudes upon official business. Since the arrival of pupils in the proper place at the proper time is rarely enough in itself to get that business going, teachers have to announce in some way that the lesson proper has begun. The boundaries of the lesson then have to be defended against intruders and defectors.(6) Pupils' full and undivided attention to the 'official environment' is most likely to be demanded at the start of a lesson, when their participation has to be 'mobilized'.(7) It is also likely to be demanded with a special firmness at the end of a lesson, on the eve of their 'demobilization'. The following examples illustrate both these common practices:

2.2   T: Right, quiet please. *Quiet* please. Er, I've tried three times for the deaf ones among us — the deaf, lame, sick, ailing, infirm . . .

Now this morning we're going into the hall because in about five minutes you'll be seeing some slides and listening to a tape. What we're going to see this morning . . . er, you two, if you can't be bothered to listen to me while I'm talking, then I don't want you in here. Now there are two reasons . . .

T: I said that we've had enough chattering. ((Pause.)) Well, I think we'll just wait another few seconds just for that absolute quiet we should have at the end of a lesson — absolute quiet. *You're* not absolutely quiet, are you, you're still talking.

Within the limits of the lesson, this demand for full attention may be frequently relaxed.(8) Unsolicited comments are tolerated or diplomatically ignored, and chattering may be allowed if it does not interfere too obviously with work. But too many side-sequences are dangerous. A teacher's discipline is judged largely by his ability to hold a class, to keep its collective attention on the matter in hand. If he fails to pass the 'order test', even in the eyes of his pupils, he is unlikely to go forward to be assessed by other criteria. The spectre of losing control therefore dissuades many teachers from risking too much 'private interaction' from which an insurrection might grow.(9) As Yeats put it, with larger disorders in mind, 'Things fall apart; the centre cannot hold; Mere anarchy is loosed upon the world'.

Despite current anxieties that things are indeed falling apart, classroom anarchy is still sufficiently rare for it to be difficult not to take for granted the general *orderliness* of the interaction. Yet if we do no more than recall that crowd of potential participants, the persistence of a central communication system should appear as remarkable. It will certainly appear so if we make an admittedly unreal contrast with what happens in everyday conversation. If only two people are talking informally together, they are likely to allow each other alternating turns. What they each get away with in the *length* of their respective contributions is clearly a complex matter, influenced (for example) by expectations arising from their previous encounters and by such immediate circumstances as one of them having information to impart or a story to tell. If more people join in the conversation, the decisions about who is to do the talking, and for how long, and about what, can become very complicated. Even with five or six gathered together, the difficulty of getting a hearing is likely to cause sub-groups to form and re-form. These may come together momentarily, perhaps while a skilful narrator holds the floor, only to disperse again once the story is told. Yet a very much larger group of pupils has to behave for considerable periods of time 'as one subordinate participant'.(10) Of course, what they are involved in is not a conversation; indeed their situation resembles conversation much less than it resembles public occasions where there is an audience and a single performer. Members of the classroom audience talk privately to their neighbours from time to time; they comment and ask questions when invited to do so; they may heckle without any invitation at all. But their main communicative role is to *listen*.

Sharp as this contrast is, it is also highly artificial. The word conversation is normally used to describe talk between equals, when there are no predetermined rights to speak first, or most, or to decide the topic. Turns at speaking have to be claimed and conceded, and what the conversation is about may change rapidly and unpredictably. These are all matters for conscious and unconscious negotiation, not for unilateral decision.(11) How does a speaker indicate his willingness to relinquish the floor to someone else? How does an intending speaker indicate his willingness to join in? How does a questioner indicate who is to answer his question? How much silence is acceptable, and whose responsibility is it to break an awkward silence? How is it made known that a topic has been talked out, and that it is time to go on to something else? In small groups, these are unlikely to be regarded as problems by the participants, however fascinatingly complex conversation analysts may find them. But in the crowded conditions of a classroom, they are *not* matters that can be improvised endlessly. There must be routine solutions available, and the relevant decisions must be made clear. That they are so can be illustrated by looking at transcripts of class teaching, including those quoted in Chapters 5 and 7. If an everyday conversation is recorded and transcribed, the participants themselves are often surprised by its apparent confusion. Utterances trail off, overlap, and are interrupted. There are frequent false starts, hesitations, and repetitions. Unedited, the result is tedious to read and often impossible to follow. In contrast, talk recorded in traditional classrooms, even without being edited, often looks like a play script. Most utterances are completed, and most speakers seem to know their lines and to recognize their turn to speak. Despite the large numbers, the talk appears more orderly. One set of obvious problems must therefore have been solved. Even in the most informal conversation, the normal rule is 'one speaker at a time'. If several speakers start together, they may refuse initially to give way. But sooner or later (and there may be a sharp battle for survival), all but one will usually abandon the floor. In classroom interaction, any competition for turns must be closely regulated. This is much easier if rights of communication are *not* shared equally — if one participant can speak whenever he chooses to do so, can normally nominate the next speaker, and can resolve any cases of confusion. In traditional classrooms, the communicative rights of teacher and pupils are very unequal indeed. To adapt Flanders's comment, which we quoted earlier, teachers usually tell pupils when to talk, what to talk about, when to stop talking, and how well they talked.

2 Participant-Structures and the Taking of Turns

Very unequal rights of speaking are apparent (conservatives may say that they used to be apparent) in most interaction between adult and child. Children may no longer need to wait to be spoken to, but adults can usually insist on their right to speak or continue speaking when they choose, to obtain a proper hearing ('Are you listening to what I'm telling you?'), to refuse to listen themselves ('Be quiet, I'm busy'), and to terminate either the whole conversation or some topic within it ('I don't want to hear another word'). None of these moves is normally available to the child. In Sacks's useful phrase, the adult can be seen as 'owning the interaction'.(12)

Teachers are very likely to 'own' classroom interaction, in these and in other ways. In so far as pupils are willing to be taught, then they are likely to concede to a competent teacher the right to talk first, last, and most; to control the content of what is said; and to control its transmission by allocating turns at speaking. The central communication system which is so prevalent in classrooms reflects and arises from the teacher's right to make most of the decisions necessary to secure orderly interaction. These decisions are apparent in the small number of patterns which can usually be seen in the talk which goes on. The term *participant-structures* refers to typical arrangements of speakers and listeners — communicative networks linking those who are in contact with one another already, or can be if they choose.(13) In traditional classrooms, the list which follows is probably in a rough order of decreasing frequency:

(1)   The teacher talking to a silent audience, and requiring everyone's attention.

(2)   The teacher talking to one pupil (asking a question, evaluating an answer, issuing a reproof), but assuming that everyone else is taking notice.

(3)   A pupil talking to the teacher, with the rest of the class as audience.

(4)   The teacher talking to one or more pupils when the others are *not* expected to listen and may be allowed to talk themselves.

(5)   Pupils discussing among themselves with the teacher as chairman (neutral or otherwise).

(6)   Pupils discussing among themselves, with the teacher absent.

It is not difficult to link these structures intuitively to certain obvious stages in lessons — for example, to the teacher lecturing, checking on the reception of the lecture, inviting queries, sorting out problems, eliciting discussion, and trusting pupils to work on their own. We consider later some of the typical exchanges associated with these stages, and how shifts from one stage to another are achieved. What even the simple list brings out is the limited variety of interactional patterns characteristic of lessons, and how firmly most of them are centred on the teacher. There is usually a formalized allocation of speaking and listening roles. Teachers expect both a 'proper' silence *and* a 'proper' willingness to talk, and they manage the interaction so as to produce orderly and relevant pupil participation. It is now time to look more closely at how this orderliness is achieved.

In a 'well-ordered' classroom, the teacher's turns at speaking are taken as and when he chooses. Teachers seem to talk less to younger pupils, to abler pupils, when they are teaching (for example) English or social studies compared with science or modern languages, and when they are regarded by their colleagues as 'superior' teachers.(14) But these variations are less striking than is the difficulty teachers generally seem to have in taking much less than a two-thirds share of the talking time. Because it involves the giving out of information, instructions, reproofs, and assessments, most of their talking can be described as *telling*. It is talk as a performance.

Such a dominant performance is usually given from a 'front of stage' location within which the teacher makes his 'footlight parade'. The metaphor is not unduly melodramatic. Many physical contexts communicate powerful messages 'from their makers to their users', and the traditional classroom settings have been both a symbol and a reinforcement of centrally controlled interaction.(15) The conventional groupings of desks or tables channel communication to and from the teacher, who is the obvious focus of attention. He can direct his talk to any part of the room, while the natural flow of pupil-talk is either to him or to other pupils through him. It is a setting which makes it difficult for the teacher to avoid talking *at* pupils, or to break up the interaction into more localized encounters. In classrooms which are physically more open, no single focus of attention may be visible at all. Symbolically and practically, there is a switch of emphasis from the teacher to the learner. Of course it would be absurd to argue that such a setting is *sufficient* to decentralize the interaction. Our point is simply that traditional classroom settings make it difficult to do so for any length of time.

Even in the traditional settings, teachers have to stop talking sometimes, not only from exhaustion but because they need regular bouts of pupil participation. Participation, or the prospect of it, mobilizes pupils' attention. It allows teachers to check on what has been learned, and pupils to display their learning. The predominant 'teaching technology' is still that of exposition interspersed with bursts of question-and-answer. But if pupil participation is therefore indispensable, it also presents formidable managerial problems because of the number of potential participants.(16) Once the teacher stops lecturing, how are turns taken? How is the rule of one speaker at a time maintained? When a question is asked, who is to 'do the answer'? These problems are normally solved by the teacher's decisions. Turns are allocated, they are not seized, and pupils have to learn to bid appropriately for the right to speak.

These will appear as statements of the obvious to any teacher. Yet the tight control often exerted over lengthy sequences of question-and-answer should make us look closely at the kind of questions which teachers typically ask. We do this in detail in the later section on the shaping of classroom meanings. But even without the pressures considered there — those of controlling the content of the lesson and maintaining topical coherence — the mere organization of the interaction makes it unlikely that many open questions can be asked. If they are to keep a single verbal encounter together, teachers cannot risk many questions to which the answers are unpredictable and which give them little or no right to close down the discussion. Instead, they must ask questions which entitle them to regain the floor frequently in order to comment on, elaborate, or evaluate the answers. The following sequence illustrates a standard teaching procedure:

2.3   T: Can you tell us what fossils are, do you think?
       P: Sir, sir, a long time ago animals — and there was animals, and when they died, er, the rain and wind came over them and then the bodies disappeared and left the shells and that.
       T: Good. Why do you think the bodies disappeared and the shells stayed?
       P: Sir, sir, they rotted.
       T: And what about the shells?
       P: Sir, they got harder — er, when the clay dried, they made marks in the clay.
       T: Right.
       P: The clay dried hard.
       T: Right, OK, thank you. Can anybody add anything to that at all? It's a very good description. Can anybody add anything to that? Yes?
       P: Sir, living creatures set in rock.
       T: Good. Now he's right in what he said in actual fact— that when these creatures were floating around in the sea . . .

The *interactional* consequences of asking questions like those about the fossils are apparent in most published examples of classroom 'discussion'. The teacher speaks before and after each pupil contribution. By getting the floor back every other turn, he is able to continue his allocation of turns at speaking, as well as to shape the meaning of what is said in the desired direction. The teacher's comment on each intermediate response indicates that a better answer is still to be attained, either by implicitly repeating the original question or by partly accepting or elaborating what the pupil has said in ways which provide some clue to what that better answer might be. By asking questions of this closed nature, the teacher is able to intervene so often that his management of the interaction should not be in doubt.(17)

Describing teachers' questions in this way leads us to look more generally at some of the managerial strategies apparent in classroom interaction. A great deal of classroom research involves some attempt to look past what teachers and pupils say to each other to what they seem to be *doing* with the words they exchange. This may be done by recording large numbers of individual 'events' (or 'acts', or 'moves') which the researcher groups together afterwards into patterns which he supposes to be significant It may also be done by trying to identify the *naturally* occurring stages through which the interaction passes, and how various moves are marked and recognized by the participants. In their different ways, both kinds of investigation have documented teachers' classroom dominance by showing how much of the communicative work is normally done by them, and how restricted are the communicative roles normally available to pupils. We have seen how most participant-structures are centred on the teacher who, within the limits of the lesson proper, either talks himself or decides who else shall do the talking. It is to some of the other evidence of this dominance that our account now turns.

3 Moves, Sequences, and Stages

One frequently quoted study of classroom interaction used the model of a language game to describe the basic moves available to the players, and how these moves were typically combined into sequences or cycles. In this game, 'the teacher sets the ground rules and acts therefore as player, coach and referee ... [he] is the most active player ... he makes the most moves; he speaks most frequently; and his speeches are usually the longest'.(18) His dominating performance was most obvious in the prevalence of one particular teaching cycle, that of 'teacher-solicit — pupil-respond — teacher-react', a sequence we have already described as the teacher taking every other turn. He also had a virtual monopoly of what were called 'structuring moves', utterances which set the stage for subsequent behaviour by indicating what the next bit of teaching was to be about. In the following exchange, that most typical of teaching cycles leads into a structuring move, and then to a further teacher-solicitation. The frequency with which such sequences are built up is a striking characteristic of classroom talk, the initiative returning frequently and regularly to the teacher.

2.4   T: Right, Anthony, can you just read through the passage to remind people of what we're doing. We'll just wait till everybody's listening. Yes, Anthony.

P: (reading) 'Arrival on the Island.' The sun was shining as the dazed passengers began to look round and see for themselves the situation they were in ...

T: Right, thanks, Anthony. Now in what Anthony's just read there are several pieces of information about the island and we've got to use those pieces of information to try to work out the shape of the island and what features there are on it ... Can anybody suggest what's the first thing that we ought to do before we start on the map? John?

P: Read through it again so we know what to do.

T: I agree with that — read through it again, but we'll ask you to do that in a minute. Before we start drawing a map of it there's something we've got to decide about the size of our map. Can anybody suggest what it is?

The reference to the teacher as both referee and player emphasizes the extent to which he can play to his *own* rules. But the analogy with a game cannot be used for long without raising formidably difficult questions about *what* verbal actions are recognized by the players as being significant moves, and *how* they are recognized to be so. Some of these difficulties are identified, though certainly not resolved, in the following chapter. What the analogy does is to draw attention to the teacher's pervasive involvement in the action. It indicates how many more moves are usually available to him, especially those moves which can be seen as *initiatives*. It is he who makes the running. As described in another, more intensive study of classroom discourse, it is the teacher who sets things going, gives *directives* and *information, elicits* responses from the pupils, offers *cues* when answers are not forthcoming, *nominates* a particular pupil to speak, *accepts* what is said as relevant, and then *evaluates* its content. The acts most often available to pupils were those labelled as *bidding* (for the teacher's attention, or a nomination to speak), *acknowledging* that they were paying attention, *replying*, and *reacting*. From the evidence of this study, there seemed to be stringent restrictions on what pupils could do with words, their talk being contained within a narrow range of communicative options.(19) That what they can *mean* is also tightly controlled is something we consider in the following section of this chapter. Concentrating still on the organization of classroom talk, we want to look more closely at an interesting feature of this study — its concern with how the boundaries of various stages in the interaction were marked. *Framing* moves were identified as those which announced that some activity had ended, and that another was about to begin. They were often initiated by the teacher's use of one or more of a limited repertoire of terms — 'Right', 'Now', 'OK', and 'Good'. *Focusing* moves defined or prepared for what the next stage was to be, so making it more likely that pupils would behave in the appropriate ways.(20) Both moves are illustrated in this extract from our own recordings:

2.5 T: Right, just listen for a second. *(A framing move, announcing that the 'proper' lesson is about to begin.)* We've only got one group in here today because the other group have gone over to the theatre, so you're on your own in the open area. Now last time we were in here, we asked you to start the new topic with a title page in your book. Now it seems a fairly easy thing to do to present the title page, and yet so many people rushed headlong into it and didn't make a good job of it. Now the reason why we tell you to do things slowly is so that you will produce good work in your book. We don't benefit from it, you do. If it's good — if it looks good, well presented, easy to read, then it's better work. Now the thing to do when you're preparing a title page is to do it in pencil first. If it's not right you can rub it out. Right? You don't scrawl a great biro line across and then realize it's wrong and then spoil it, you think ahead and plan. Correct?

Pn: Correct.

T: Thank you. Now after that *(first focusing move — or set of moves — completed)* you should all choose the booklet that you're going to start on and then begin work. Now apart from Abdul, who I'm going to help in a second, is there anyone here who doesn't know what they've got to do next? *(A further focusing move, with a check on its effectiveness which reveals a few more unable to 'carry on'.)* . . . Now does that mean that everybody else except Peter, Paul, Abdul, and Shirley can carry on? (Pause.) Right. *(Framing move, announcing that 'everybody else' is now to 'carry on'.)*

The frequency of such moves in classrooms is explained by the way one of the participants is managing the interaction of the others, and perhaps is only gradually revealing the significance of their activities. The moves can be seen as part of a larger strategy by which this management is achieved — that of providing a running commentary on what has happened, is happening, and is about to happen.

In any prolonged discourse, orderliness and coherence will sometimes depend on the speakers' talking about the talk in various ways. For example, they may comment on the taking of turns ('Can I just get a word in here?'), or on the kind of turn just taken ('Are you serious?'), or on whether their listeners are indeed 'getting the message'. Only in the most routine conversations are the participants unlikely to be at least occasionally surprised by, or uncertain about, what is said. At other times, they will need occasional reassurance about where the conversation is going and occasional instructions about how it is to be organized. When the necessary directions are put into words rather than hinted at in other ways, they can be described as *metacommunication*, a monitoring of talk by talking about it. Now in most verbal interaction, this monitoring is a shared responsibility, though the sharing may well be unequal. The hostess at a party, for example, has to keep a special watch for prolonged silences or disruptive arguments, while the doctor in the consulting room has to ensure that he gets enough of the right information.(21) What is unusual about classrooms is not only that so many *metastatements* are made, but also that they are almost all made by the teacher. Indeed, Michael Stubbs has suggested that they constitute a very large part of what teaching *is*.(22) We have seen already some of the reasons why this might be so. Teachers have to separate the lesson proper from the surrounding 'unofficial' talk. Pupils may arrive on time, and display some visible signs of a willingness to learn (they go to the right place in the room, they carry the right books, and they may even open these books without prompting), but they can still do many things that are not 'learning' until the official beginning is announced, and private activities previously tolerated are marked in some way as being interruptions or disruptions. Within the lesson, there will also be stages with perhaps some sharply differing rules about the appropriate quantity, distribution and forms of talk, and teachers have to provide the relevant 'stage directions'. Stubbs' detailed account of this monitoring process includes various categories of metastatement which we found it easy to illustrate from the lessons we observed:

(1) *Attracting attention* — 'Girls, it might be a nasty rumour, but I've been told you're doing nothing.'

(2) *Controlling the amount and distribution of talk* — 'You're making too much noise at this table, you should be working.'
'Hang on, let's have a girl. Sylvia come on, you seem to be willing to talk.'

(3) *Specifying the topic* — 'We're going to look at the people on a small island, how they solve the problems of shelter, food, clothing, law and order — you know, the problems we looked at before half term.'

(4) *Checking or confirming understanding* — 'Is there anyone who doesn't know how to work out a map now? Nobody? Well, that's great, we've done well this morning.'

(5) *Correcting and 'editing' what is said* — 'Why will the eagle go for that one?'
''Cos it can't fly.'
'Well, no, it can fly — that's not the reason.'
''Cos it's white.'
'Yes, because it's white. Why will it go for it because it's white?'
'It can see it better.'
'That's right, in that environment the other one is better *adapted*, it's — what's the word?'
'Camouflaged.'

(6) *Summarizing* — 'So from a story from long ago we've used that story to work out how people thought about themselves, how they lived.'

Of course, pupils do some of these things too. They often check that they have the teacher's attention or have understood an instruction, and they offer their own interpretations of their conduct or of what part of the lesson has been about. But if their metastatements become so frequent that they provide an alternative source of directions and definitions, then a very untypical situation has arisen. Since it is the teacher's responsibility to carry through the official business, it is the teacher's talk that essentially constitutes the lesson.

The monitoring of talk was described earlier as a running commentary on what is happening, has happened, and is about to happen. To extend the metaphor, teachers often talk their pupils through the 'action'. But this analogy would be highly misleading if it suggested a clear distinction between events and statements-about-events. By offering an explicit definition (or redefinition) of what is being done with words, a metastatement can constitute the event itself. In everyday conversation, the interactional significance of most of what is said is likely to be taken for granted, and frequent demands to know precisely what the other means will be regarded as pedantic or even offensive.(23) But if communication seems to be breaking down, or conflict arising, then some monitoring of the talk becomes necessary (e.g. 'I find that remark insulting'; 'I was only joking'). In unequal relationships, this process may be very one-sided, with the superior insisting on *his* right to establish what has really been taking place. Since the meaning of most pieces of interaction can be formulated in many ways, this can be a formidable advantage. Teachers habitually insist on *their* definitions of situations and events. They do so, for example, when they translate or edit a pupil's contribution into a more convenient form ('What you're really saying is that . . . '). They do so when they identify a particular contribution as being impertinent, irrelevant, honestly mistaken, or downright silly. Being at the centre of the interaction, they have extensive powers of selection in the behaviour, and in the meanings, which they choose to take up for explicit notice and comment. To restate the general point, 'an insult which is not *recognized* as an insult is not, interpersonally, an insult'; teachers can therefore treat flippant remarks as genuine contributions to class discussion, making the best of them and fighting hard to uphold their definition.(24) They can sometimes avoid a serious confrontation with pupils by recognizing a potentially serious challenge as infringing only a relatively minor rule, while by persistently assuming in what they say that pupils already share their own definitions of events, they routinely announce and reinforce the official version of what is really taking place.(25)

In the rest of this chapter, we concentrate on the shaping of classroom meanings in relation to the transmission of official *curriculum* knowledge. But before doing so, we make a final organizational comment. The descriptions of classroom interaction already outlined present essentially similar profiles of the teacher's dominance. Teachers are mainly talkers, sometimes the target for the talk of others, rarely just one of the audience. Most teacher-talk can be described as 'telling'. Teachers make most of the communicative moves, forcing the other 'players' to respond rather than allowing them to launch initiatives of their own. Their allocation of turns maintains an orderly interaction, their questions enable them to maintain topical coherence by persistently evaluating what pupils say, and their running commentary provides authoritative definitions of what is taking place. These typical features of classroom interaction both reflect and reinforce a particular model of teaching, and it is a model which researchers of various methodological persuasions strongly dislike. But whatever educational objections may be made to it, we believe that it confronts many teachers with an increasingly difficult managerial task. Our somewhat abstract account of how classroom talk is organized makes the teacher's control appear too easily gained and too easily held. Yet to keep so many potential participants together in a single communication system for so much of the time is an extraordinary achievement because nothing like it *of such duration* can be found in any other context. Even when the teacher's authority was supposedly less questioned than it is now, it was an achievement which imposed great strain. In Waller's memorable phrase, the authority of teachers was 'a despotism in a state of perilous equilibrium'. In today's schools, especially in urban areas, the perils are greater and the equilibrium more unstable. The imposition of a single verbal encounter for large parts of most lessons is an obvious source of trouble because it generates so many acts of at least minor deviance — acts like not listening, chattering, and shouting out. Teachers need pupil participation, but they have to control it; they need enough, but not too much.(26) Some pupils will want to participate because they have something to say, and many more want to do so from time to time so as to display themselves as good learners. In conditions of conventional class teaching, they have to compete for scarce resources of communicational space, they may have to do so according to a strict etiquette of how to bid for permission to speak, and they have to balance the risks of being too strident against the risks of being squeezed out of the 'official' talk altogether. For long periods of time, they have to curb their natural verbal ebullience. In short, they suffer from an excess of communicational demand over supply, in market conditions operated by a single controller. Such conditions generate disaffection, and they partly define the forms its expression will take.

4 The Shaping of Meaning in Classroom Interaction

So far in this chapter, we have separated the management of classrooms from the management of the knowledge being transmitted. This may seem to treat the teacher's control as a purely organizational matter of keeping order, and of course there are times when teachers themselves see things in this way. In especially taxing circumstances, they may adopt a custodial approach simply to survive.(27) This transformation of means into ends obviously loses sight of the instructional tasks which justify the teacher's control. Means and ends are, nevertheless, inseparable. We agree strongly with Douglas Barnes that the forms of communication which predominate in classrooms make up a large part of *what* is learned there(28), and we will return repeatedly to the inseparability of what is said, and how it is said, from the social relationships in which the speech is embedded. In classrooms, it is their position as knowledge experts which justifies teachers in 'owning the interaction'. To the extent that their expertise is acknowledged, they will be expected to do most of the talking themselves, and to evaluate what is said by others. The transmission of knowledge creates and sustains very unequal communicative rights between teachers and learners. Knowledge is already there to be passed on, the teacher knows how much of it he intends to transmit in a given time, and interaction is organized to facilitate its reception. But before examining more closely how this controlled transmission is achieved, we turn to some of the constraints on meaning which are imposed by the public nature of so much classroom talk.

(a) Formality and social distance

Formality is difficult to escape in interaction so obviously managed from the centre. Many accounts of classroom life describe the relationship of teacher and pupils as one in which personal feelings are largely subordinated to the tasks in hand, the respective roles being seen as filters through which most personal information is screened out. Flanders has called classrooms an 'affectional desert' because almost *all* the talk there is devoted to official business, and even teaching which is cognitively stimulating has been described as leaving no room for passion and emotion.(29) This is not to say that the talk expresses nothing of the relationships involved, but rather that the expressive information being transmitted is about the proper role behaviour of teacher and pupils and very rarely about individuals' feelings of friendliness, hostility, boredom, or intellectual excitement. Some of the consequences for teachers were described by Waller as 'the didactic voice . . . the voice of authority and the voice of ennui. There is in it no emotion, no wonder, no question and no argument. It imparts facts. There enters likewise into the classroom

voice the voice of command . . . This tone of voice goes with a formaliza-
tion of all social relationships and a stereotyping of the *words* of
command.'(30)

Waller's assertions might stimulate teachers to reflect on voice production, though they imply a wealth of supporting evidence which did
not, and does not, exist. There is no doubt that a great deal of social
information is carried in the way things are said, but (as we will see in the
next chapter) the task of identifying *how* it gets into speech is extremely
difficult. The whole notion of formality, which we have already used
without explanation, is much easier to recognize intuitively than it is to
define and document. Waller clearly associated it with impersonality
and social distance, and with relationships between superiors and sub-
ordinates, and it is along these two dimensions of solidarity and power
that one relatively straightforward means of transmitting social information has been studied. When they address each other, do speakers
exchange last names and titles, or use the respectful form of 'you' in
languages which contain that distinction? If they do, it would suggest a
relationship which is not intimate, and may be unequal. Does one of
them use the relaxed form, but receive the polite one? Such asymmetrical
usage suggests a hierarchical relationship.(31) In classrooms, modes of
address are usually asymmetrical. When a teacher insists on his surname
and title, or on 'Sir' or 'Miss', then this is one way of announcing and
maintaining distance which is repeated so often as to become part of the
habitual definition of the relationship. The reciprocated first-names
allowed by some teachers, and generally encouraged in some schools,
symbolize and may reinforce more personalized interaction. There are
some interesting variations too, such as the old practice in mixed classes
of using first-names to girls only, and the consequent opportunity to use
the full name as a reproof ('Mary Jones — I will *not* tell you again').
Teachers may also use first-names or nicknames, and receive their
first-name, to mark the temporary informality of a classroom (or, more
commonly, a sports field) encounter.

These examples remind us that the way things are said often signals
nuances or changes in relationship. Although he saw it as difficult to
escape for long, Waller's 'didactic voice' appeared in the context of a
range of voices employed by teachers, the 'voice of command' being
occasionally replaced by 'that tone of voice which is completely human,
completely personal, and entirely relaxed'. More readily observed than
are intangible qualities of pitch and intonation, the transition from one
stage of a lesson to another (for example, from lecture to discussion) may
be marked by a *general* change to a more colloquial style.(32) Humour is
another obvious resource for achieving such relaxation. Opportunities

for 'having a laugh' rank highly in pupils' assessments of teachers, and the laughter is often subversive of official business, providing an 'antidote to schooling'. But jokes are often used by teachers as an 'instrument of policy' — to release tension, relieve boredom, signal their solidarity with their pupils, or simply to 'appear human'.(33) As such, and used judiciously, they facilitate control. But in most classrooms, they represent occasional departures from a prevailing formality. As Waller observed, 'those who live by controlling others must take thought even of their laughter'. In schools as they were formerly constituted, teachers had to 'keep state in order to keep control'. The alternative was the strain of having endlessly to 're-create' their leadership in conditions in which it could never be taken for granted. For most of the time, Waller argued, the relationship of teachers and pupils was necessarily impersonal. If it was important to know how to relax that relationship, it was also important to be able to tighten it again at need. Formality in voice, word, and phrase were important resources for maintaining and restoring social distance, and Waller described in some detail the conventional 'buffer phrases' which teachers often used to do so.(34) We would suggest that one of the difficulties new teachers experience is that of restoring an appropriate level of businesslike formality once they have allowed pupils to approach too closely.

More recent accounts of boundary marking have extended the analysis to include more general questions about language and social control. Predominantly formal ways of speaking are still seen as keeping teachers and pupils at arm's length, but in the larger sense of setting classroom life apart from the everyday world. When Susan Houston, for example, writes about *classroom register*, she identifies a range of styles which includes the kind of language expected of those in authority, but which excludes the everyday language of many children. This register serves to align the classroom with the dominant culture, and to handicap outsiders.(35) The assumption that respectably standard speech is somehow intrinsically better suited to the serious business of learning has been a matter for heated debate. What is certain is that children who find it difficult to speak in ways approaching that of their teachers, or who refuse to do so, often find it difficult to have *what* they say taken seriously.(36) A persistent linguistic gulf between them may also mark the estrangement of the two worlds of home and school. We return to this point when we consider in Chapter 3 the special 'languages' associated with particular areas of the curriculum.

The repeated references to the impersonality of classroom language remind us that much of the talk is public in the most obvious sense of that word. So much of what is said is said to an audience. The possible scorn

of their fellows is in itself unlikely to encourage pupils to take risks in stating their opinions or presenting what they know. Caution is even more tempting when whatever they say will be evaluated by the teacher, and treated as evidence of successful or unsuccessful learning. The Bullock Committee argued that children should learn in school to cope with the public presentation of information and ideas. But it also suggested that less formal contexts are necessary to encourage thinking aloud. On the 'stage' encountered in traditional class teaching, children are likely to say what is safe. In small groups, and in the company of those they know well, the talk is more likely to be 'tentative, discursive, inexplicit and uncertain of direction . . . The intimacy of the context allows this to happen without strain. In an atmosphere of tolerance, or hesitant formulation and co-operative effort, the children can "stretch" their language to accommodate their own second thoughts and the opinions of others.'(37) While a public setting undoubtedly encourages safe statements of the obvious, a more private setting is of course no guarantee of a full and frank exchange of views. There may be strong pressures within the intimate group towards conformity with the opinions of others, and so towards an easy and premature consensus. But while informal groups are not a sufficient cause of exploratory talk, traditional class teaching is unlikely to provide the necessary conditions to support it. The public and centralized nature of the talk provides some of the reasons why this is so. Other reasons lie in that 'vertical' transmission of knowledge to which we referred earlier, and to which we now return.

(b) The persistence of the 'recitation'

> Any schoolchild playing teacher will produce most of the behaviour used by most teachers. Typical behaviours are: standing in front of a group of relatively passive onlookers . . . doing most of the talking . . . asking questions to which they already know the answers . . . and evaluating by passing judgements.(38)

If this is indeed what playing teacher means, then children's everyday knowledge closely resembles what classroom research has shown to be the predominant teaching technology. Many descriptions of teacher behaviour have been based on polarized models reflecting the extent of teacher dominance (for example, dominative/ integrative, authoritarian/ democratic, closed/ open, direct/ indirect), and have reported typical performances as falling heavily on the directive side. These models represent various ways of talking about that main teaching strategy which has been called the 'recitation'.(39) The term refers not to lecturing in the ordinary sense of that word, but to exposition interrupted by questions. An authoritative version of the facts is intro-

duced by the teacher, developed through leading questions which channel discussion in the right direction, then tidied up and summarized.
Where courses have been built around a more neutral teaching role,
teachers have found it difficult to employ a merely procedural authority
and to renounce the expert's right to control the content as well as the
form of discussion. This new role has seemed difficult to enter, and
certainly to maintain, because teachers are 'more authoritarian than
they realize'.(40) Much of this authoritarianism arises from emphasizing the transmission of knowledge from those who know to those who do
not. Clear boundaries between knowledge and ignorance mark the
pupils' main role as that of receiver. In relation to the knowledge being
handed down, their own existing knowledge is regarded as slight, partial, or defective. They have to step into the teacher's meaning system,
and leave it relatively undisturbed.(41)

In its extreme form, the recitation is an exposition by the teacher in
which gaps are left for pupils to fill with *exactly* the information he would
otherwise provide himself. But it is more likely that what pupils say will
be elaborated and modified so that it fits more neatly into the developing
exposition. Teachers are less likely to listen *to* what is said than they are
to listen *for* what they can use and what they should discard. Because
they know what they want to hear, they offer 'assessments' rather than
'replies', and these assessments are likely to contain more or less explicit
clues to what a better answer might be.(42) This evaluative feedback, so
prevalent in traditional teaching, is not only essential as a way of
recognizing success and failure in learning; it is also an essential part of
the learning process itself. It is therefore necessary to look again, and
from this perspective, at the kinds of question which teachers typically
ask.

(c) Classroom questions and the managing of answers

To ask a question in ordinary conversation is, for the moment, to take the
initiative. Someone, often specifically assigned the responsibility, has to
answer the question, and since a response obviously unrelated to it
would cause offence, the question defines what the next part of the
conversation is to be about. But if the questioner is genuinely seeking
information, his display of ignorance may soon *lose* him the initiative
because it opens the way to a possibly lengthy exposition by someone
who does know the facts. Having handed over the communicative
responsibility, the questioner may well not get it back. While he may be
obliged to acknowledge the answer, and even comment on it, his initial
ignorance rarely entitles him to evaluate or correct its content except to
indicate whether or not he has been told enough. But things may not be

so straightforward. The question may be rhetorical. The questioner may be a secret expert in the very matter he has raised, and asked his question to provide a feed-line for himself. Asking pseudo-questions is often a way of regaining the floor next-turn-but-one.(43) The question identifies the *listeners'* ignorance, perhaps arouses their curiosity, and then justifies the questioner in answering it himself.

This tricky device is not uncommon in everyday conversation. It is uncommonly common in classrooms. For despite the departures from normal form which have just been outlined, it is not usual in conversation to ask questions to which you already know the answer; ask obvious questions, the answers to which should be known by any competent member of the group; ask questions without making it clear what you want to know; or ask questions without making it clear how much you want to know. Most of the questions asked by teachers, however, seem to do these very things. Since they rarely seem to arouse either bewilderment or hostility, then very different rules must apply to what such questions are for, and to the form which appropriate answers should take.

Teachers often ask obvious questions, the answers to which are either 'common knowledge' (common to 'any' child of that age, or of that level of ability, or to 'any' student of that subject at that stage of his career), or else have already and perhaps very recently been provided in what pupils should have heard or read. Such questions serve as a check on attention, a failure to answer them demonstrating not a lack of ability but a failure to participate. They also define the minimum level of competence expected of *those* pupils in *those* circumstances.

Teachers usually ask questions to which they already know the answers, whether they indicate this in the form of the question or in the way they respond to the replies. There may be only one right answer and one correct formulation of it, or pupils may be permitted to express 'the' answer in their own words, or a limited range of alternative answers may be available. In all these degrees of closure, the answers are contained within authoritative limits which have been predetermined by the teacher, and the function of the questions is to test whether or not pupils are operating within the teacher's frame of reference.(44)

We referred earlier to the interactional consequences of closed questions, especially to the frequency of sequences in which the teacher speaks every other time. We are concerned here with the shaping of meaning, and one obviously relevant consequence is that even when the questions are lengthy, pupils' replies are often very short. Questions eliciting information which the asker can be presumed to know already both invite and justify inexplicit answers. This is especially so when the answers are so frequently elaborated. For it is what teachers do *after* a pupil has replied which makes classroom questioning so distinctive. Each reply is normally followed by a comment from the teacher, not necessarily on the correctness of what was said, but certainly on its relevance. Indeed, in the early stages of the search for an answer, explicit evaluations may be witheld so as to encourage participation, and to elicit suggestions which will at least outline the *area* of search. But pupils accustomed to traditional teaching are likely to be bewildered into silence if the teacher witholds evaluation for too long, because they will be looking for some verbal assurance that they are on the right track. Of course, there will be clues to what the answer is in pupils' knowledge of what questions in that particular subject are likely to be about, in the level of difficulty expected of their ability, and in the residues of past lessons from which they can fill out what the question means. But more immediate resources of information are likely to be provided by the teacher as the lesson proceeds, so that when the answer at last emerges he can be said to have 'managed' it.(45) The following extract neatly illustrates the process because both teacher and pupil make it explicit:

2.6   T: But what is it that makes a housing shortage in some parts of Britain?
      P: The bricks?
      T: No.
      P: The land?
      T: No. ((There follows a prolonged exchange in which the pupil tests out various answers relating to the *making* of houses, presumably because of previous work on Tristan da Cunha where people normally made their own, and the teacher eventually tells him to think about those living in them.))
      T: Look, forget about the houses and think about who's going to live in them.
      P: The people who build them.
      T: The people who build houses are going to live in them? In *this* country? We're on about this country now, remember.
      P: Oh, in *this* country — oh, we get people who build them.
      T: But why is it that in some places there are not enough houses for the number of people in that place?
      P: There are not a lot of workers.
      T: No.
      P: They've got vandalism?
      T: No — *don't think of it from* — *you're thinking of it from the one end*, the houses.
      P: *Which end do you want us to think from?*
      T: *I want you to think of it from the other end*, which is the number of people. (Italics added here are *our* emphasis.)
      P: Yes, 'cos there's a lot of people — too many people after one house.
      T: *Right*, in some areas there's simply too many people for the number of

houses available. Now on Tristan are there too many people? How many people are there?

P: 300.

T: Right, so at any one time the actual number of people who need to build themselves a new house is very small, and then with people dying off as well that means that a house becomes available for somebody. OK? So that's why there's no problem over housing.

If the search for the answer becomes too prolonged, as it was in this exchange, the clues are likely to become increasingly specific until the goal is reached. In the earlier stages, they have to be inexplicit enough to give some reality to the search, and yet sufficiently clear for the track not to be lost altogether.

It is important not to make this shaping of meaning look either too straightforward or too ruthlessly efficient. It is often unclear until some way into a lesson what that lesson is about; indeed, an entire lesson can sometimes be interpreted as an exercise in progressive demystification.(46) Teachers' questions often refer back to items of information which were not marked out at the time as being especially significant, and they often leave it unclear how much information is necessary for an answer to be adequate. Answers are often rejected, or accepted without any positive approval, with no explicit indication of the grounds for doing so, while pupils who do pass the test are not always sure what the test was. Teachers often seem to operate with several concurrent standards of correctness, and there are sound pedagogical reasons for this, such as a readiness to adapt their responses to the abilities of individual pupils, or to tactical objectives within some larger strategy.(47) But the resulting 'inconsistencies' may lead pupils to depend even more heavily on clues which the teacher provides, rather than on what they might work out from their own resources. These clues are an important outcome of that selective listening to which we referred earlier in the chapter, and to the monitoring of classroom talk as it proceeds. The brevity of so many pupil contributions opens the way to such extensive elaborations of what they said that they can no longer recognize the idea as their own. By filling in what (in both senses of the word) he *presumes* to be the meaning behind what was stated so briefly, the teacher can reflect back his own version.(48) Pupils too are often adept at leading teachers on in this way so that they finish by doing the hard work themselves.

It is the teacher, then, who normally controls what is and can be meant in the classroom. The restricted range of communicative options open to pupils is therefore inseparable from the restricted range of *semantic* options. Though they often ask for procedural clarifications and for further clues, pupils rarely take the semantic initiative by posing

related to meaning in language.

questions or volunteering information from outside the teacher's frame of reference. What they can mean is normally bounded by what the teacher considers to be relevant, appropriate, and correct. Differences between one transmission classroom and another are likely to be differences only on the surface, leaving the basic structure of the interaction undisturbed. Now in arguing in this way, we are aware of the danger of drawing too sharp a contrast between active talking and passive listening, for listeners too may be actively involved in constructing new meanings for themselves,(49) But open classrooms are supposed to display more manifestly active pupil roles, and there are very few recorded examples to which to refer.(50) One of the fullest is the account by Massialas and Zevin of what they call 'dialectical' teaching. While the 'didactic' teacher does all the things we have described already, the 'dialectical' teacher 'legitimizes creative expression' by declining to act as the authority. He does not lecture, or plant clues, or ask leading questions, or evaluate answers. As far as possible, pupils are thrown back on their own resources, and their own sense of the quality of their inquiries, and the teacher is a *participant* in the search for answers.(51) But descriptions of such teaching are rare. There are other reasons why most classroom research has been done in traditional classrooms, but one reason has undoubtedly been the scarcity of significant alternatives. What the best-known studies of classroom interaction have done, in their different ways, is to show what most teaching has essentially been like.

Chapter 2: Notes and References

1   The Bullock Report, *A Language for Life* (1975), p. 142.
2   Visual styles of learning are well described by John (1971), 'Language and Educability', in Leacock (ed.), *The Culture of Poverty*. See also Cole *et al.* (1971), *The Cultural Context of Learning and Thinking*. Both studies discuss the problems of adjustment facing children who suddenly encounter in classrooms a preponderance of verbally presented information. The resistance of American-Indian students to 'normal' rules of classroom communication is described in the chapters by Dumont and Philips (1972) in Cazden *et al.* (eds), *The Functions of Language in the Classroom*.
3   All the classroom examples in this chapter are taken from our own research. As in later chapters, the following conventions are used: Pn = two or more pupils speaking together; italics = raised voice; 'Can you . . . . ' = speech tails off; : : : : = stretch of interaction omitted; ( ) = words guessed or indecipherable; (( )) = observer descriptions.
4   Barnes and Todd (1977), *Communication and Learning in Small Groups*, p. 1.
5   Adams and Biddle (1970), *Realities of Teaching*, p. 3.
6   The clear physical boundaries characteristic of conventional classrooms

help to confine pupils' attention. Disturbances to which more open class-rooms are vulnerable are described in Stebbins (1973), 'Physical Context Influences on Behaviour', *Environment and Behaviour* 5(3).

7   Hammersley (1976), 'The Mobilization of Pupil Attention', in Hammersley and Woods (eds), *The Process of Schooling*.

8   Permitted and uncorrected 'side-involvements', together with other forms of what he calls 'away behaviour', are described in Goffman (1963), *Behaviour in Public Places*, pp. 69–75.

9   Walker and Adelman (1975b), *A Guide to Classroom Observation*, define infor-mal teaching as occurring when the teacher is willing *not* to know what is going on everywhere. It is then the single verbal encounter which is likely to be transitory. Our reference to the 'order test' comes from Gannaway (1976), 'Making Sense of School', in Stubbs and Delamont (eds), *Explora-tions in Classroom Observation*. He suggests that the next tests are 'Can we have a laugh?', and 'Does he/she understand us?'. There is some support for this order of priorities in Furlong's chapter in the same book, and in Woods (1976b), 'Pupils' Views of School', *Educ. Review* 28.

10   Hammersley (1974), 'The Organization of Pupil Participation', *Soc. Rev.* 22.

11   Conversational analysis has become a special area of academic interest, especially for ethnomethodologists. See e.g. the chapters by Sacks, Scheg-loff, and Speier in Sudnow (1972), *Studies in Social Interaction*; and Speier (1973), *How to Observe Face-to-Face Communication*.

12   Speier (1976), 'The Child as Conversationalist', in Hammersley and Woods (eds), op. cit. Speier quotes Sacks's reference to 'owning' interaction.

13   Philips (1972), 'Participant-Structures and Communicative Competence', in Cazden *et al.* (eds), op. cit.

14   Systematic classroom observation has provided extensive factual support for this statement, e.g. the chapters in Amidon and Hough (1970), *Interaction Analysis*, by Furst and Amidon, Amidon and Giammateo, and Amidon and Flanders.

15   Stebbins (1973), 'Physical Context Influences on Behaviour', op. cit.; Get-zels (1974), 'Images of the Classroom and Visions of the Learner', *School Review* 82.

16   Hammersley (1976), op. cit., defines teaching technology as strategies 'collectively produced and sustained rather than idiosyncratic'. The sus-tained preeminence of lecture-and-question is described in Hoetker and Ahlbrand (1969), 'The Persistence of the Recitation', *Amer. Educ. Res. Journal* 6.

17   Managing the interaction in this way is well described in Hammersley (1977), 'School Learning: The Cultural Resources Required by Pupils to Answer a Teacher's Question', in Woods and Hammersley (eds), *School Experience*.

18   Bellack *et al.* (1966), *The Language of the Classroom*, p. 238.

19   Sinclair and Coulthard (1975), *Towards an Analysis of Discourse*.

20   It is interesting to compare these moves with the notion of switch-signals developed by Hargreaves *et al.* (1975), *Deviance in Classrooms*.

21   Very asymmetrical monitoring of talk is described in Coulthard and Ashby (1975), 'Talking with the Doctor', *J. of Communication*.

22   Stubbs (1976a), 'Keeping in Touch: Some Functions of Teacher Talk', in Stubbs and Delamont (eds), op. cit.

23   Indignation deliberately aroused by demands to clarify the meaning of obviously commonplace remarks is described in Garfinkel (1964), 'Studies in the Routine Grounds of Everyday Activities', *Social Problems* 11.

24   Wegman (1976), 'Classroom Discipline: An Exercise in the Maintenance of Social Reality', *Soc. of Educ.* 49.

25   Torode (1976), 'Teachers' Talk and Classroom Discipline', in Stubbs and Delamont (eds), op. cit. In his interviews with teachers, Stebbins found a tendency to define ambiguous conduct by pupils as though it were disorderly, and to find difficulties in responding to some behaviour initiated by pupils. But when teachers took the initiative, they usually assumed that pupils saw things as they did. See Stebbins (1975), *Teachers and Meaning*, pp. 55, 83–4.

26   Hammersley (1974) and Hammersley (1976), op. cit.; Westbury (1973), 'Conventional Classrooms, "Open" Classrooms, and the Technology of Teaching', *J. Curr. Studies* 5. The 'singular success' of the 'recitation' is seen by Westbury as a coping strategy. In large groups of often unwilling pupils, and often lacking supportive resources, it enables teachers to secure some pupil participation and yet retain control over the interaction and its content. But, as Hargreaves *et al.* (1975) suggest, it also generates a large number of rules to be broken.

27   Stebbins (1975), op. cit., pp. 91–4; see also Woods (1977), 'Teaching for Survival', in Woods and Hammersley (eds), op. cit.

28   Barnes (1976), *From Communication to Curriculum*.

29   Jones (1968), *Fantasy and Feeling in Education*, pp. 24–5. Entries in the first category of Flanders's own observation schedule — 'accepts feeling' — are usually extremely sparse. Adams and Biddle (1970), op. cit., comment on their own classroom research that 'the time spent on sociation was so minimal that it need not be discussed'.

30   Waller (1965), *The Sociology of Teaching*, p. 229. Waller might well have included this depressing prediction in his later discussion of 'What teaching does to teachers'.

31   There is an excellent review of such studies by Ervin-Tripp (1972) in Pride and Holmes (eds), *Sociolinguistics*, pp. 225–40.

32   There is a clear illustration of this in Fishman and Salmon (1972), 'What Has the Sociology of Language to Say to the Teacher?', in Cazden *et al.* (eds), op. cit., where Swabian high-school teachers are described as descending from standard German to the regional vernacular when they move from lecture to discussion.

33   Woods (1976a), 'Having a Laugh: An Antidote to Schooling', in Hammersley and Woods (eds), op. cit. Many observation schedules used in classroom research contain categories like 'warms (informalizes) the climate . . . (e.g.) jokes that release tension'. One of the advantages of a central communication system is that a stock of shared jokes can be built up to which the teacher can refer implicitly; see e.g. Walker and Adelman (1976), 'Strawberries', in Stubbs and Delamont (eds), op. cit.

34   Waller (1965), op. cit., pp. 189–233 and 279–89.

35 Houston (1970), 'A Re-Examination of Some Assumptions about the Language of Disadvantaged Children', *Child Development* 41. For an extended treatment of the controversy, see Trudgill (1975), *Accent, Dialect and the School*.

36 Edwards (1976), *Language in Culture and Class*, chapter 4.

37 The Bullock Report (1975), op. cit. This section of the Report seems to summarize the views of Douglas Barnes, who was one of the expert witnesses. Barnes's own investigation of small-group talk is reported in Barnes and Todd (1977), op. cit.

38 Simon and Boyer (1970), *Mirrors for Behaviour*, p. 2. This is a collection of systems for observing classroom behaviour.

39 Hoetker and Ahlbrand (1969), op. cit.; Barnes and Shemilt (1973), 'Transmission and Interpretation', *Educ. Review* 26; Nuthall and Snook (1973), 'Contemporary Models of Teaching', in Travers (ed.), *Second Handbook of Research on Teaching*.

40 Stenhouse (1969), 'Open-Minded Teaching', *New Society* 14 and Stenhouse (1973). 'The Humanities Project', in Butcher and Pont (eds), *Educational Research in Britain* 3. Stenhouse's comment could be supported by two recent studies of Nuffield Science teaching, Eggleston *et al.* (1976), *Processes and Products of Science Teaching*, and Cooper (1976), *Bernstein's Codes: A Classroom Study*.

41 Cooper (1976), op. cit. For a discussion of knowledge boundaries in relation to history teaching, see Edwards (1978), 'The Language of History and the Communication of Historical Knowledge', in Dickinson and Lee (eds), *History Teaching and Historical Understanding*.

42 Barnes (1976), op. cit., p. 111. In discussing his category, 'Teacher uses pupil's idea', Flanders recognizes the difficulty of distinguishing between a use of it in a form which the pupil would still recognize as his own, and an extensive translation of it to fit the teacher's ideas.

43 Waller (1965), op. cit., pp. 289−90 gives a witty account of such verbal 'grappling hooks'.

44 The openness of questions is usefully defined by Barnes and Todd (1977), op. cit., p. 126, in terms of the relative authority of the questioner and answerer. Research suggesting a predominance of closed questions in classrooms is reviewed in Edwards (1976), op. cit., chapter 5. Of course, much that is taught in schools *is* a matter of right and wrong answers. But several studies have shown teachers closing down discussion even on controversial issues; see e.g. Bellack *et al.* (1966), op. cit., and Kliebard (1966), 'Dimensions of Meaning in Classroom Discourse', *J. Teacher Educ.* 17.

45 Hammersley (1977), op. cit. Some of the clues obtained from categories of subject matter and ability are discussed in Keddie (1971), 'Classroom Knowledge', in Young (ed.), *Knowledge and Control*.

46 Hammersley (1976) and Hammersley (1977), op. cit.

47 Mehan (1974), 'Accomplishing Classroom Lessons', in Cicourel *et al.*, *Language Use and School Performance*.

48 This taking over and reconstruction of children's responses is described in the context of ability testing in Leiter (1974), 'Ad Hocing in the Schools', in Cicourel *et al.*, op. cit.

49   This point is well made in Wight (1976), 'Speech Acts, Thought Acts', *Educ. Review* 28.

50   Many systematic studies of classroom interaction have tried to identify 'certain kinds of highly desirable intellectual performance' and then to work back to the kinds of teacher and pupil behaviour which preceded it: Gallagher and Aschner (1963), 'A Preliminary Report on Analyses of Classroom Interaction', *Merrill-Palmer Quart.* 9; see also Ober *et al.* (1971), *Systematic Observation of Teaching*; Smith and Meux (1970), *The Logic of Teaching*; Hunter (1972), *Encounter in the Classroom*, chapter 5.

51   Massialas and Zevin (1967), *Creative Encounters in the Classroom*.

Chapter 3

Analysing Classroom Talk

Introduction

In the conventional model of scientific research, meticulous experiment and observation provide objective data from which theories can be derived and by which they can be tested. Scientifically-minded investigators of the social world may also assume that they have access to some part of the real world that they can pin down and dissect. From this perspective, the path to a science of teaching lies through the collection of objective data, the systematic testing of relationships of cause and effect, and the gradual accumulation of well-tested knowledge.(1)

By describing typical patterns of classroom interaction, and what teachers do to create and maintain them, we were conforming in the last chapter to normal research procedure, outlining what is already known as a base for advancing into some new territory. But that evidence was presented uncritically. Although it had been collected in a variety of forms by a variety of methods, it was simply added together to portray what research 'has shown', as though the diversity of facts were facts of the same, or of a compatible, kind. This procedure is justified if we assume that different approaches to research will uncover, more or less competently, different aspects of the same reality. But what the researcher sees may be largely determined by what he is 'set' to see. A particular view of what constitutes reality then provides the facts necessary to justify it, and different realities are constructed according to the perspective adopted.

Too sharp a contrast is being drawn here between the objective scientist remorselessly revealing hard facts, and the blinkered observer bringing back only what he expected to find. The first image exceeds the claims of even the 'hardest' social scientist, while the second suggests such an infinite variety of truths that it transforms social science into a species of fiction. Our own approach lies between these artificially polarized positions, though considerably nearer the second. We are concerned in this chapter with how classroom interaction appears from different vantage points. It was suggested in the Introduction that teachers lack 'an adequate descriptive language for talking about their own professional behaviour'. In fact, though none may be adequate, there are many such languages available. In comparing them, we are *not* assuming the existence of a single reality to which some of these descriptions correspond. Our immediate aim is to show how different accounts of classroom talk are generated because of the stance which the researcher takes. Conventionally, a social scientific theory is seen as being tested in a crucible of hard facts — facts which are independent of that theory and which will show it neither fear nor favour. This separation of theory from data is quite unrealistic. It may be useful at times to distinguish between observation 'explicitly limited by an observer's subjectively acquired theory', and observation which 'at least attempts to resist theoretical shackles for as long as possible'.(2) But theory is not something *apart from* observation, to be seen either as shackling the researcher or as showing him how to make sense *afterwards* of what he first saw with an innocent eye. Whatever description of social life is presented is itself the outcome of selective observation as well as interpretation, theory determining not only how the data are to be explained but also what are to count as data in the first place. What are facts from one perspective will be ignored from another.(3)

What we do in this chapter is to gather some representative studies of classroom talk under three broad headings, recognizing that each compartment will still contain very diverse contents. We then examine what sort of facts these studies produced, and why they did so. We also look at some of the distinctive problems which confront researchers of different kinds. Such an approach risks being merely destructive, indicating difficulties so zealously as to suggest the futility of doing any research at all. But however critical our tone, it is not that of spectators comfortably safe from having to join the game. We are reviewing the conceptual ground-clearing undertaken before beginning our own classroom observation. This metaphor may suggest a necessary preliminary to gathering some useful crop, but it may also suggest mere devastation. Because we naturally incline to the first alternative, the chapter is increasingly pointed towards the methods we decided to use ourselves. Our intention is not to survey the ground impartially but (like the teacher with his closed questions) to extract what is useful for our purposes and throw the 'husks' away.

1 What is Done with Words: The Systematic Approach

Most of the time in classrooms, someone is talking. In the most common form of classroom research, that of systematic observation, a manageable record of what is said depends on extracting the essential features from an otherwise overwhelming stream of talk. This is usually done by coding the talk into a number of categories which are claimed to abstract these essentials from the surrounding noise. The interaction can then be 'tallied and plotted on a matrix to present an objective picture of the verbal patterns' so that 'systems for analysing classroom talk can tell us what actually occurs in classrooms'.(4)

The reliability of the most widely used category systems is not in doubt. That is, they allow 'any trained person who follows stated procedures to observe, record and analyse interactions with the assurance that others viewing the same situation would agree to a great extent with his recorded sequence of behaviours'.(5) The observer knows what he is looking for, and he produces precise and quantifiable data relevant to his purposes. But the larger question is obviously that of validity. Similarly trained observers may agree with each other, but *are* they seeing what really occurred?

This question of validity draws attention to the theories underlying systematic observation, because the categories represent preconceived ideas about what is really important in classroom interaction. Though the theoretical positions are often inexplicit, they can usually be described as broadly behaviourist.(6) The criteria for classification refer to observable effects and not to the intentions of the actors, and the basic model of interaction is one of stimulus and response. Indeed, a behaviourist stance is sometimes made very explicit indeed, classrooms being viewed in terms of specific teacher-behaviours which bring identifiably predictable results or even as 'a laboratory in which a continuous complex of experiments is constantly going on'.(7) Even when the assumption is not spelled out, the teacher's verbal behaviour is seen as largely determining what occurs. Though many researchers of this kind claim to be simply *describing* the patterns of verbal interaction characteristic of classrooms, some reforming zeal is usually apparent, and so is a confidence that feeding information back to teachers about their behaviour at certain critical points will enable them to get things the way they want. To believe that this can be done is to believe that the information provided has indeed captured the essence of the interaction.

On what is this confidence based? Although they are rarely articulated by those who rely on them, a number of methodological assumptions must underlie this kind of research. Some systematic studies have used videotape recording, so making it possible to refer to non-verbal cues to meaning. But most observers rely on the words alone. They assume that the verbal behaviour is a sufficient sample of the total behaviour — that any non-verbal communication necessary to generate and sustain class-room interaction is either subsumed in, or subordinate to, what is actually said.(8) If only because of the difficulty and expense of collecting non-verbal data, this is an assumption common to most approaches to classroom research. Certain other assumptions, however, would be challenged by researchers adopting a sociolinguistic or ethnographic perspective. An outline of what they object to provides a useful bridge to examining these alternative approaches to making sense of classroom interaction.

Some systematic researchers make recordings of what is said so that they can code it retrospectively. But it is more usual to categorize the talk as it occurs. It must therefore be assumed that the meaning of what is said can be instantly recognized — that the trained observer acts 'like an automatic device, albeit a highly discriminating one' and codes the talk unhesitatingly 'at the instant an event is recognised'.(9) Now in our earlier discussion of metastatements, we referred to the many categories available in everyday language for treating separate actions and utterances as being essentially the same (for example, as jokes, insults, or complaints). These categories often relate to language itself. Was an utterance a question, a statement, or a command? If it can be broadly classified as a command, was it an order, a request, or an appeal? If certain ways of saying things always meant the same thing — for example, if commands were always expressed in the imperative form of the verb, or questions in the interrogative — then there would be no problem. But of course, they do not. Some of the categories used in classroom research may *seem* obvious enough, as when a teacher is recorded as 'lecturing' or 'correcting'. Others, however, depend on a high level of inference, as when the observer has to distinguish genuine praise from a mere verbal habit, or recognize that the teacher is 'warming the climate'. Even for what might seem a straightforward identification task, a dedicated behaviourist still finds it necessary to provide 'functional guide-lines' to when a question is indeed a question.(10) Systematic researchers are usually blind to the complex problems of matching form and function. They have also ignored a matter of critical importance to many social scientists — the relationship between how an observer categorizes what he sees, and how the participants themselves identified the events. We know of no systematic studies in which the observer's understanding of what was said was checked with the teacher and pupils involved. Indeed, the logic of the approach denies the need for such checking. The observer is trained to notice those acts included in his category system, and to ignore irrelevances. His attention is therefore highly selective. Since the participants have so much else to attend to, and no reason to regard those preselected acts as especially noteworthy, their accounts might well differ from the observer's record without undermining his confidence. He knows what he was looking for, and he would also know that similarly trained observers would confirm *his* version. But, as we have suggested already, the undoubted reliability of category systems is no answer to allegations of a *predetermined* consensus. Events can be said to have occurred in so far as trained observers will agree that they did so. But since their common frame of reference provides its own solutions, or guide-lines, to most problems of interpretation, it can be argued that references to the accuracy or correctness of the record relate solely to this view from the outside. Things might have appeared very differently both to the participants *and* to observers armed with a different theory.

In many varieties of systematic observation, the problem of identifying what is being done with particular sequences of words is intensified because the observer has to assign an interactional significance to utterances as they occur. In all but the most ritualized interaction, the construction of meaning is far too provisional and dynamic for this to be possible. Talk is not one distinct item after another. It involves what has been called 'conditional relevance'; the meaning of an utterance arises partly from something else which has been (or will be) said, perhaps some distance away in the interaction, in relation to which it is understood.(11) Listeners refer back to what was said earlier, or wait to see what is said next, before deciding what the speaker really means. This point, of great importance for our own analysis of classroom talk, can be illustrated by considering a problem facing many systematic researchers, that of distinguishing between closed and open questions. A closed (or narrow) question might be defined as one to which the correct response can be predicted, and this predictability *may* be apparent in the form of the question (e.g. 'What is the date of the Battle of Hastings?', or 'What happens when you add sulphuric acid to zinc?'). But many questions which appear to be open are closed because of the context in which they are asked (perhaps the teacher has recently provided 'the' answer), or because the teacher has clear criteria of relevance or adequacy or correctness of expression to which he refers in evaluating the answers. The narrowness of the question only appears in what happens next, in the way the teacher responds to what is said by excluding possible alternatives.(12) It will be necessary, then, to wait and see, or to recall what was said before in order to make sense of what is being said now. As we ourselves will clarify later in the chapter, a neglect of sequencing in verbal interaction has been a main criticism of systematic classroom research.

Our argument so far may have implied a greater reliance on form alone than is actually practised. Systematic researchers do not assume that the form of what is said is normally unambiguous; rather, they assume that what is done with words in classrooms is so distinctive that it can be readily identified by observers who know what classrooms are like. It is for this reason that they can cope with the rapid succession of coding decisions which have to be made. Up to a point, as we will see, this assumption also underlies some sociolinguistic investigations of classroom talk. But these would certainly not share the systematic observer's confidence that he can recognize at once what is happening at that stage of the interaction. Even in typical classrooms, this confidence is excessive.

Some of the criticisms we have outlined might be dismissed as reflecting an esoteric preoccupation with theory, and systematic approaches defended on the grounds that they work. As Flanders argues, his system should *not* be seen as a contribution to theory, but as a 'tool of action'. The information provided by systems like his is provided quickly and cheaply; because there is nothing mysterious about them, teachers can be easily trained to apply them to their own or their colleagues' lessons; and typical patterns of verbal interaction can be plotted so as to make it possible to work back from some desirable outcome to the behaviours that preceded it. What outcomes *are* desirable are for the teacher to decide. Though the purpose of researchers like Flanders is to discover teaching-acts associated with high pupil motivation and achievement, and though a strong preference for indirect methods is usually apparent, the main category systems are presented as offering the means towards a variety of ends.(13) Such practical objectives are evident in a detailed description of one of the most widely used systems as being designed to 'help teachers move away from tradition and blind experimentation toward intelligent control of their verbal behaviour', thereby making their teaching 'less accidental, haphazard and routine'.(14) Teachers could improve their teaching by so selecting their verbal behaviour that 'their practice will be what they intend'. It is not surprising, then, that the systematic approach has been so influential in teacher training, or that its apparent usefulness has attracted far more generous research funds than its rivals.(15) There is no doubt that it can provide a rapid record of the distribution of talk, and of (for example) initiatives and responses between teacher and pupils. Consulting such a record, the teacher may then decide to talk less, so leaving more communicative space for others, or to use more indirect influence by reducing his lecturing and asking fewer narrow questions. Certain patterns of verbal interaction can be associated with certain desirable learning strategies, with at least the implication of cause and effect.(16) Flanders, for example, has identified 'critical teaching behaviours' with 'measurably probable' consequences. One such critical moment is when a pupil has just answered a question. What should the teacher do next if he wants a genuine discussion? As we saw earlier, what he *is* likely to do is to elaborate and evaluate the answer himself, transforming it from the pupil's property into his own. What he might do instead is to *use* the idea on its own terms, as a peg for further pupil contributions ('That's an interesting point — what do the rest of you think?'), or perhaps refrain from speaking at all in the hope that the resulting pause will be ended by the original contributor speaking again, or by a spontaneous response from another pupil.(17)

Now if systematic observation can provide evidence of the effectiveness of such changes in teacher behaviour, do the worries of its critics matter? They matter in so far as they indicate severe limitations on what it can contribute to our understanding of classroom interaction. Remorselessly abstracting 'events' from the stream of words, it greatly underestimates both the complexity and the fluidity of what happens. It also tends to make teaching look altogether too easy. Of course, the kind of evidence it provides can be treated as a preliminary to more subtle investigation, and the organization of the previous chapter might imply this since the early description of a central communication system relied heavily on systematic research.(18) But we have already suggested some theoretical reasons for regarding such research as incompatible with the approaches examined in the rest of this chapter, and we conclude the section with some severely practical objections.

Systematic researchers rarely say much about the physical setting of the interaction they observed, about the history of the relationships involved, or about the wider school context. The meagreness of the background information might be justified by the objectivity of the methods. If the categories are free from any assumptions about the intentions of the actors, then prior acquaintance with them is unnecessary. And if the essential dimensions of classroom interaction have been identified already, then category systems can be used in (or easily adapted to) almost any classroom, regardless of subject matter or the age and ability of the pupils. Even if this were so, they cannot be used with any type of teaching. They depend on a predominantly public exchange of information, on the existence of something like a central communication system. They usually have to be packed away when nothing resembling transmission teaching is available to be recorded — for example, in the more physically active, less centralized contexts found in many primary schools. The apparent dominance of transmission teaching, and the ubiquity of Flanders's 'rule of two-thirds', may have been exaggerated by what has been the main approach to classroom research. These are the classrooms we know most about because these are the classrooms which are most easily known. It could also be argued that in so far as most teaching has been like this, it has had the research methods it deserved. The more allusive, fragmented, and personalized talk occurring in informal classrooms could not be captured by an observer newly arrived with his observation schedule.

This argument has been developed at length by Walker and Adelman, and we largely accept it.(19) In informal classrooms, there is much less of that traditional division between performer and audience, and much less public talk to which everyone should attend. Many of the meanings being exchanged will make sense only to members of the small groups involved. Indeed, teacher and pupils in any classroom build up a large store of restricted meanings — anecdotes, jokes, or insults which were spelled out in some past interaction and are then alluded to again and again. These are part of a 'common culture' which the stranger observing them cannot share. He has access only to the bare bones of meaning, 'the universals freely available in our culture'. The argument is persuasive, though it rather ignores that level of meaning which might be described as lying between what is available to 'anyone in the culture' and what is entirely local to that group. These are the meanings which are typical in situations *of that kind*. It is also important not to underestimate the extent to which meanings are private even in traditional classrooms. If systematic observation lacks a sense of place, it also lacks a sense of time. Thus their interest in how a 'silent language' of shared meanings was gradually constructed by teacher and pupils led Smith and Geoffrey to question correlational studies of teacher- and pupil-behaviour on the grounds that the critical influences at some particular moment might be 'the residual by-products of past interaction', and so would not be visible to an observer who had not shared the history of the relationships involved.(20)

Some of these arguments will be elaborated in the rest of this chapter. In doing so, we have to admit that alternative approaches are likely to appear more difficult and less scientific, and that they are usually *much* more expensive in time. In so far as systematic observation works, it does so by deliberately simplifying the phenomena it records. If alternative approaches confront the complexities of classroom interaction more boldly, do they therefore provide any greater insights into what happens? They may be theoretically more interesting, but do *they* work? We return to these questions in the final chapter. There are certainly risks in any large move away from what has been the mainstream of classroom research. But we believe that a little bewilderment is preferable to a calm assurance that it is possible to categorize, count, and account for, what 'really occurred'.

2 Sociolinguistic Perspectives: The Forms and Functions of Classroom Language

Some systematic researchers are openly atheoretical, while others draw heavily on learning theory or group dynamics for social scientific support. Both varieties, however, present their work mainly as a source of practical guidance for teachers. In contrast, sociolinguistic investigations of classroom talk have often been more concerned with advancing theory than with influencing practice, and so are presented not as 'applied' but as 'basic' research.(21)

Evidence reported in the previous chapter suggests why this has been so. Sociolinguists are interested in how speech is organized in contexts which are 'typical, recurrent and repeatedly observable', and in 'that part of language behaviour that can be related to social factors and stated in these terms'.(22) Language is studied to see how it is organized to serve certain social purposes, and social relationships are studied to see how they are 'realized' linguistically. Such investigations are easier, or they will appear easier, where the constraints on what can be said, and how it can be said, are strong and obvious. In classrooms, for example, it might well be thought that 'teacher-pupil relationships are sufficiently well defined for us to expect clear evidence of this in the text'.(23) It was because they confidently expected such 'clear evidence' that Sinclair and Coulthard began their search for generalizable methods of discourse analysis by making an intensive study of the language of teachers and pupils. Avoiding what they called 'ordinary, desultory conversation' as the 'least overtly rule-governed form of discourse', they looked instead for situations with 'clearly recognizable roles, objectives and conventions'. As we saw earlier, some social scientists *are* interested in ordinary conversation because they want to see how matters like turn-taking and topic-switching are negotiated between equals. Sociolinguists like Sinclair and Coulthard are either more interested in, or only feel able to cope with, situations in which there are predetermined rights to (for example) talk first, last, and most, to interrupt, and to decide what the talk is to be about.(24) Informal classrooms were also avoided because a greater equality between participants made the talk too much like conversation. In traditional classrooms, a clear structure of 'roles and objectives' would be recognizable in what was said, so that many 'potentially ambiguous utterances' would be likely *in that context* to have 'one accepted meaning.'

Some of the strengths and difficulties of this situational approach are what concern us in this section. In particular, we are interested in that problem identified earlier as the matching of form and function.

(a) Speaking appropriately

In describing and accounting for typical classroom interaction, sociolinguistic researchers often have in mind some notion of situational competence. Colloquially, competence refers to being good at (or adequate at) something. In the sense in which it is being used here, it refers to that knowledge of what can and should be done which underlies what *is* done. The more general concept of *communicative competence* includes knowledge of language itself (vocabulary, grammar, and so on), and of rules regarding its use; it refers to forms of speech *and* ways of speaking.(25) Some ways of speaking are associated with particular kinds of situation, and someone who does not know the relevant communicative etiquette risks having what he says ignored, misunderstood, or not taken seriously, however grammatically correct it may be. He also risks being written off himself, or at best having allowances made for him as someone obviously inexperienced in that kind of situation. It is in this area of research that sociolinguistics has been most impressive theoretically *and* most obviously relevant to the work of the schools. In emphasizing that a common language does not guarantee shared ways of speaking, it has indicated significant discontinuities between the forms and uses of language which predominate in schools, and those experienced by many children in their home world. The following example of such research was chosen because of its relevance to our earlier account of centralized classroom communication.

Learning to behave 'properly' in classrooms is very much a matter of knowing when as well as how to speak. By comparing typical participant-structures in classrooms with those apparent on no less public occasions in the community outside, Susan Philips offers a persuasive description of the discontinuity between 'mainstream' teachers and American-Indian students. In their own community, the students were not accustomed to a formalized distinction between performer and audience, or to being required to talk or to listen on demand. They therefore seemed most at home in classrooms where they could work in groups with no obvious leader, and where they could initiate contacts with the teacher when they felt the need to do so. Where they had to listen to long expositions, talk in their proper turn, and talk mainly to the teacher, they became increasingly reluctant to talk at all. They might then fail to obey an order or answer a question, not because they had failed to understand what had been said, but because they did not share the teacher's assumption that the use of an imperative or interrogative form by someone in authority implied 'an automatic and immediate response from the person to whom they were addressed'. What Philips fails to make clear is whether not sharing the situationally relevant rules was a matter of ignorance, or of knowing but rejecting them. If these students' frequent silence was an expression of resistance to the teacher's demands, and perhaps of a deeper resistance to being converted to the mainstream of American society, then instruction in the appropriate communicative behaviour would achieve nothing. 'Why don't they talk more in class?' is a very political question, and Philips's answers to it are understandably ambivalent. She recognizes the need to work *with* different ways of speaking in a culturally diverse society, and to avoid making false inferences about ability from some of the differences which become apparent. But she also sees formal classroom learning as requiring teacher-centred participant-structures to which students have to conform if they are to succeed.(26) Where the emphasis is strongly on the transmission of knowledge, she is probably right.

That single account of communicative discontinuity and conflict highlights a question which is fundamental to sociolinguistic analysis of typical situations, as it is to any account of apparently routine social interaction. Does competent participation simply mean knowing what the relevant rules are and applying them, the immediate situation being treated as an instance of some general category? If the participants then apply the same rules in the same (or compatible) ways, orderly interaction can begin and be maintained. It should also be possible for an observer who knows the situation to predict what forms that interaction will take — for example, what participant-structures will predominate, or what level of formality is likely to be employed. Certain identifiable social constraints will then be visible in the text, which 'is meaningful not so much because we do *not* know what the speaker is going to say . . . as because we do know'.(27)

Classrooms have seemed well suited to this kind of analysis, which involves treating them as settings in which many features of the talk can be seen as 'both patterned and predictable on the basis of certain features of the local social system'.(28) But there are also good reasons for caution in adopting an approach which can easily become over-determined. Two of these reasons will only be mentioned briefly, because they are elaborated in the final section of the chapter. Even in the most status-marked settings, some of the talk will be extra-contextual; that is, as a prelude or a postlude or a diversion from official business, it will be unaffected by otherwise relevant constraints. Difficulties also emerge in dealing with the official talk once it is realized that the situation which the participants recognize rarely involves a single set of constraints and possibilities, or a once-and-for-all orientation to the 'proper' forms of speech. Rather, there is likely to be a continuous processing of contextual information, involving frequent and rapid adjustments to different phases in the interaction. This second reason suggests a process far more active than simply following the relevant rules. Our own heading itself implies such conformity. But constraints are also resources. What sociolinguists call *unmarked usage* describes ways of speaking which are normal in those circumstances, and which therefore confirm the status quo. They may be so normal as not to be noticed at all. *Marked usage* is unusual in those circumstances, and so it will be noticed. Listeners may interpret it as evidence of the speaker's incompetence. But they may also recognize it as a deliberate challenge to the normal forms of social relationship, or as an attempt to redefine the situation and the kind of interaction which should take place. On occasion, then, competence will include knowing what to do to speak *in*appropriately. Susan Philips's account rightly emphasized control as well as conformity, and this double perspective is useful in considering both what we referred to earlier as *classroom register* and also the specialized forms of speech associated with particular areas of the curriculum.

Because speaking formally is a powerful means of maintaining social distance and of impersonalizing relationships, pupils are often expected to show respect for learning, and for their teachers, by avoiding speech that is too colloquial. The whole business of schooling may also be so strongly associated with a single, 'standard' variety of language that a convention comes to seem a necessity and it becomes difficult to regard as scholars (or aspiring scholars) those who speak in very different ways. Speaking inappropriately with intent can then be an expression of hostility to teachers, or an assertion of the pupils' own cultural identity against that represented by the school. But consistently non-standard speech can also be an unwitting source of disadvantage, not because such speech is inherently inferior as an instrument of thought but because it is so easily read as evidence of low ability or of an unwillingness to move into the teacher's frame of reference. Of course, pupils whose habitual form of speech is far removed from that thought proper in classrooms are often adept at switching codes. But where they are unable (or unwilling) to do this, they risk being taken at best 'for a good-natured clod or an honest peasant'.(29) In documenting various forms and sources of interference between the languages of home and school, sociolinguistic research has shown how disadvantaged children from some social groups will be if the speech forms with which they are most at ease are pointedly excluded from the classroom, and if the purposes to which they normally put their language are rarely encountered there.(30)

A similar analysis can be made of 'subject languages', though detailed evidence is still so scarce that it can only be a matter of applying some general ideas to these specialized contexts. The distinctive forms of speech (and sometimes writing) associated with many social groups serve two main functions. They make it possible to conduct 'business' more efficiently by providing means of communication which are both brief *and* precise, and they also symbolize membership of the group and loyalty to it. There are times when to 'talk like one of us' is to *be* 'one of us', even when the relevant 'language' may consist of little more than a few items of vocabulary.(31) The 'language of' academic subjects can be seen in this way — as a mixture of intellectual necessity and group solidarity. The necessity arises from the development of special terms for objects and ideas of special, perhaps even unique, importance to that discipline. But many more esoteric terms are used than are strictly necessary. This additional usage has been called conventional rather than intellectual, though any implication that they are merely verbal habits would be misleading. Both necessary and conventional usage serve to mark off some special area of interest, and teachers' frequent preoccupation with the right terminology (even when it is hard for an observer to see what the fuss is about) is a way of indicating the separation of academic from everyday knowledge, or of one academic territory from another. When a word makes some discrimination which in everyday language is either not made at all or is 'polluted' with other meanings, then teachers cannot afford to tolerate apparent differences in meaning between themselves and their pupils. They have to insist on their definition of what is a technical term in their subject. If such intolerance extends to semi-technical (or pseudo-technical) usage, it is because one way of indicating what is and is not relevant is to talk about things in a special way. As pupils come to do so in ways which fellow specialists can recognize and accept, they reinforce their sense of belonging to that field of knowledge.

(b) Structures and functions

From a purely linguistic perspective, references to the 'language of' school subjects greatly exaggerate the extent and the frequency of the differences being identified. Our *socio*linguistic account has emphasized the significance of specialist usage — how it functions to announce and reinforce a particular academic reality. Such an account reflects what has been described as the main task of sociolinguistics, that of identifying social functions and then discovering what linguistic features are selected and grouped together to serve them.(32) The task is intricate and troublesome. We often know intuitively when and how this service is being performed, but a confident identification of ways and means is another matter altogether. As was suggested in Chapter 2, relatively straightforward examples can be found in the use of forms of address to express social distance or deference, or to signal a temporary relaxation in a normally formal relationship. The double attraction of studying them is that the range of available options is usually small (e.g. 'Do I use full name or first name?'), and that the choice often seems to provide clear evidence of how the speakers perceive their relationship. But what other forms of linguistic service can be recognized? *How* something is said is often a large part of *what* is said, but could the speakers themselves define (let alone an observer recognize) what forms were performing what functions at a particular point in the interaction?

The difficulties of doing so are illustrated in two over-confident attempts to work on fine details of classroom talk. In a comparison of three classrooms, Mishler tries to show how different teaching strategies were 'carried' in the structure of the teachers' speech, his larger theoretical purpose being to identify 'the social functions of particular forms of language'.(33) For example, the most open teacher frequently used tentative forms of expression, while the most directive tended to present words as though they had fixed meanings. Now these items may have been significant in the circumstances in which they were recorded, but it is not at all clear that they were as important as much more obvious features like the amount of pupil-talk or the kind of questions asked. The tentative *form* in which a question is asked may be quickly contradicted by a dogmatic evaluation of the answer. We accept Mishler's argument that so little is known about the functions of particular linguistic features that an investigation like his has to to range widely, but his own reliance on various items as hard evidence is too bold. Simply, there are too many ways of saying the same thing, while the same items may convey quite different meanings in different contexts. Though he would probably accept that cautionary note, Torode argues that the actual words exchanged are 'the only reality with which an analysis of speech should be concerned'. Because those words convey definitions of the situation, they can be taken as evi-

dence of what is obvious to the participants.(34) In his analysis of
how one teacher keeps order and another fails to do so, Torode pays
close attention to how they use the pronouns 'we', 'you', and 'I' to
define the relevant 'persons' and relationships in their interaction
with pupils. The strong teacher is able to use them consistently, and
to locate them within a firm structure of orderly activity to which he
and his pupils are subject. The weak teacher offers no clear definition either of the immediate interaction or of the wider context, and
the persons he defines are only loosely identified and related. All this
and more Torode claims to extract from the use of pronouns. But it
is not the appeal to specific pieces of evidence which is persuasive.
What his account suggests is that the weak teacher is unable to secure and maintain typical *classroom* talk. Because his exchanges with
pupils remain at the level of ordinary conversation, they lack centralized control and they display an 'improper' participant-equality. But
this is our interpretation rather than his, and it represents a general
impression of the interaction rather than a firm diagnosis precisely
linked to the structures of teachers' and pupils' speech.

Our comments on these two studies may appear solely destructive.
But what we are arguing against is too close a causal matching of
structures and functions. There are fundamental reasons why
attempts to treat fine details of talk as hard evidence will rarely be
productive. Even in the most typical of situations, there is 'almost no
correlation between the *linguistic* distinctiveness of relevant variables
and the social information they carry', and no way of specifying in
advance the nature and size of the critical signals.(35) To complicate
matters much further, the social significance of 'relevant variables'
may well vary with different phases in the interaction, and they are
also likely to be serving several functions simultaneously. These
complications remind us again that speech cannot be separated from
other aspects of social behaviour and then correlated as though they
were different levels of reality. Social facts which might be used to
explain features of linguistic choice — facts like the roles of 'teacher'
and 'pupil' — are not obvious and permanent qualities of speakers.
They often have to be announced and confirmed in the course of
interaction. Speaking 'out of role' may itself informalize the relationship, while using appropriately deferential forms of speech signals an
unequal relationship *in the act of speaking*.(36) Our own position can
be summarized by juxtaposing two comments of Michael Halliday.
Behavioural strategies will undoubtedly be realized 'somewhere' in
the linguistic system, but 'a sociological theory could not operate
with raw speech fragments as the only linguistic exponents of its

fundamental ideas'. Speech may take the *form* it does because of
what it is being used to do, but it is extremely difficult to identify
this happening. Halliday's own work has increasingly emphasized
not the appropriate forms of language, but the semantic options
which are typically available. He has therefore described contexts
where what the participants can mean 'is rather closely specifiable'.(37) Although he has not included classrooms in this analysis,
much of the research cited in Chapter 2 indicates a 'meaning potential' which is subject to very one-sided processes of definition. What
pupils can mean is normally determined by what the teacher treats
as being relevant, appropriate, and correct. The teacher's expert
knowledge acts selectively on what is said and how it is said, and
tracing the communicative and semantic options typically available
in classrooms is therefore a research task of great importance.

One recent attempt to carry it out is much more convincing than
Mishler's because of an explicit abandonment of stylistic markers as
hard evidence of what was going on. Barnes and Todd chose instead to
describe in more functional ways how pupils expressed their sense of
control over how the problems confronting them were defined, and over
the knowledge relevant to their solution.(38) Normally, the teacher's
authority provides a framework within which classroom talk is organized *and* classroom meanings are controlled. He has 'acknowledged
responsibility for the direction of the discourse, for deciding who shall
speak when, and for introducing and ending topics',(39) and when
things are going smoothly many of the relevant decisions will not be put
into words at all. There is a special value, then, in studying how orderly
and coherent interaction is achieved in educational settings when the
teacher is *not* there to direct and manage, and when the necessary
monitoring has to be shared. Exploratory talk between pupils resembles
conversation in that there are few predetermined rights to control either
topics or turns. Not only are meanings being constructed rather than
being transmitted ready made, but the social relationships necessary for
doing so also have to be negotiated and renegotiated. When the resulting
talk can be described as collaborative, evidence for that description *may*
be found in *how* things are said — in intonational and other ways of
indicating that what is said is open to question and challenge (for
example, frequent use of 'may', 'perhaps', 'possibly', and of 'I *think*'
rather than 'I think'). But many formal markers of uncertainty can be
verbal habits, and they can be contradicted by what the speaker is
dogmatically *doing* in the interaction. Barnes and Todd concentrated
instead on how pupils initiated, elicited, modified, questioned, recalled,
and summarized their respective contributions. In communicative con-

ditions very different from those generated by transmission teaching, what were those pupils able to do, and to mean, with the words they used?

3 Sociological Perspectives: Classroom Contexts and Classroom Meanings

The terms 'structure' and 'function' are typical markers of the sociologist at work. Our repeated use of them in the previous section indicates the artificiality of separating sociolinguistic and sociological perspectives on 'language in context'. There are large overlaps in approach, and common interests in showing (for example) how things are done through talk, how the significance of words as acts is often tied to the particular context in which the words are spoken, and how certain utterances (and therefore actions) may be tied to certain social identities or positions.(40)

The shared interest which especially concerns us here is in the situational embedding of meaning. Our earlier discussion of situational competence emphasized the importance of knowing how to speak, when to speak, and how to use speech, in various typical contexts. We turn now to how speakers make use of that knowledge to communicate much more than they *say*, and to fill out the meaning of what is said to them. It is this knowledge which an outsider will lack. Observing, for example, an informal classroom which does not conform to the traditional type, he 'cannot understand what is being said in a way that allows him to hear the talk as it is heard by the pupils'. He may pick up many standard meanings, but 'he misses the meanings available only to a participant in the relationship'.(41)

It was a wish to capture this view from the inside which drew sociologists belatedly into classroom research. Using the observational techniques of the anthropologist, they tried to portray the realities of classroom life as these appeared to the teachers and pupils involved.(42) In doing so, they had to confront problems which systematic observers disregard, especially the relationship between the observer's view of events and the views of the members. How far could the observer share in the situational competence of those he observed, and so make the same kind of sense as they did of what occurred? A researcher confronting this question is likely to feel it necessary to immerse himself in the life of the group, and to do so over a considerable period of time. A famous example of such prolonged immersion, though mainly psychological in orientation, is the account by Smith and Geoffrey of the complexities of an urban classroom as these were seen and *jointly* interpreted by teacher and researcher. They claim to have been unsure what it was they were getting up to until someone suggested that they were engaged in the 'microethnography of a classroom'. They were then delighted to adopt this impressive label. What it meant in practice was a detailed account of the 'grooving-in' of new pupils to ways of behaviour which they would gradually come to see as what is and ought to be done in that context. As the year went on, these descriptions and prescriptions became matters of increasingly *im*plicit reference — a 'silent language' cumulatively constructed and used. The observation of its construction took Smith into all Geoffrey's lessons for an entire school year, and such heavy expenditure of time is a characteristic of ethnographic research. Furlong, for example, needed a longer period of more intermittent observation to record how a small group of girls participated in and made sense of classroom events, while Torode saw almost all the lessons of one class for six months in his efforts to get away from simply labelling a teacher's performance to showing what was involved in giving the performance.(43)

Studies like these contrast sharply with a systematic observer's analysis of (let us say) forty social studies lessons in forty classrooms, and they often have the vivid appeal of attempts to 'tell it like it is'. Our own preference for *in*tensive observation will be apparent throughout the rest of this book, and it arises partly from a criticism of systematic observation which was outlined earlier — its lack of a sense of place and time. So much of what is said in any context 'cannot be understood apart from the context, and the context cannot be read by those who do not share the history of the relationship'.(44)

Meaning is embedded in its context in so far as speakers use that context as a taken-for-granted background to what is actually said. They use what *is* said as an index to (or as a document of) a much larger set of meanings, filling in these appropriate meanings by interpreting what they hear and relying on others doing the same when they speak themselves.(45) Hearing an utterance which is not immediately intelligible, they refer to their knowledge of the situation to narrow the range of possible meanings and perhaps to authorize one particular interpretation. What is meant on that occasion may depend on who the speaker is, on when and where he is speaking, and on his relationship to the listener. Assertions, requests, commands, pleas, and so on are often recognized as much from the context in which they are delivered as from the form in which they are expressed. As we commented earlier, classrooms have appealed to some sociolinguistic researchers for just this reason — because utterances which might otherwise be ambiguous are clarified by knowing what teachers and pupils typically mean, the structure of teacher-pupil relationships providing a basis for assigning meaning to what is said. For example, if a *teacher* says, 'Is that someone talking in the back?' the words are more likely to be interpreted as a command for silence than as a question requiring a verbal answer, despite the interrogative *form*. If he says, 'Would you please open your books?' his pupils are unlikely to perceive an option of not doing so, despite the formal tentativeness of the request. Such contextualized interpretations depend on the participants' knowing what normal teacher-pupil interaction is like. Of course, it is always possible for the *immediate* context to be misread, and for a pupil to mistake a genuine question ('Jane, why are you laughing?') for a command to pay attention. But the mistake arises partly from knowing the typical function of such an utterance.

Reference to the *immediate* situation reminds us again that context should not be used as an ill-defined and static dumping-ground for what the participants are supposed to know about that part of their social world. The relevant context changes rapidly. Lessons have various stages or phases, often with quite specific rules of communication in operation within them, and often with routine ways of marking their boundaries.(46) We noted earlier the frequency of framing and focusing moves by teachers as part of their general responsibility for monitoring classroom talk. But identifying such moves is only part of the researcher's larger task — that of showing how teachers and pupils make known and sustain a common definition of what is going on at different points in their interaction. If the situation is often changing, then they will need frequent evidence that they are indeed understanding each other. Talk is the main source of such reassurance. They will have to perceive and transmit the information necessary to sustain orderly interaction and, in doing so, to identify and use the relevant context. The researcher's problem is how far he shares their knowledge so that he too can follow what is going on. The attraction of classrooms for many researchers — the relatively overt structure of the interaction — has perhaps been dangerous in leading them to underestimate the amount of work the participants have to do to sustain that interaction *and* the work the observer has to do to make sense of what occurs. In their study of informal classrooms, Walker and Adelman describe some of the technical difficulties they faced as being inseparable from 'general questions about the kinds of information certain situations require to exist, and about the minimum perceptions and transmissions of that information required to constitute and sustain identities within them'.(47) What do the participants need to 'perceive, recollect and express' in order to interact competently? How are they to code the relevant social information? What do they have to know to recover information which is not carried on the surface of what is said? But these are questions which should be asked by researchers in all kinds of classrooms. They direct attention to *how* situations are talked into existence, and to how far an outsider can penetrate those meanings which are embedded in the context.

Extensive reliance on a back-cloth of shared meanings to support and fill out what *is* put into words rests on the participants' assumption that each is seeing the situation in broadly similar ways — that there is a *reciprocity of perspectives*. Indeed, those who know one another (or that kind of situation) will implicitly *demand* 'embedded expressions to ensure and reaffirm the existence of past relationships'. (48) To talk to someone as an insider is to make him an insider, while to spell out what everyone knows is to treat listeners as either outsiders or incompetents. Now in classrooms, teachers tend to assume that *their* meanings are shared — that when they initiate interaction (as they usually do), pupils are seeing things in their terms, or are willing to learn how to do so. This assumption allows them to act without reflection for much of the time, experiencing difficulty in defining the situation only with interaction initiated by pupils. They also tend to define ambiguous pupil-behaviour as though it was disorderly.(49) When they are making the running themselves, they trade heavily on pupils' knowledge of the 'silent language' of the classroom. The implicit forms of speech which result have the obvious advantage of enabling them to avoid making their authority too obtrusive too often. For example, in announcing a deviant act, they have somehow to identify the offender, the rule which has been broken, the action which is breaking that rule, and the conduct which will restore conformity to it. It is rare for all four components to be stated explicitly, and not uncommon for none of them to be.(50) In this and other ways, teachers and pupils rely on common knowledge to fill out the meaning of what is said, and spell out what they mean only when they have evidence that understanding has broken down or when something is going to be different. The point has been neatly illustrated in a detailed comparison of a conventional teaching encounter with one in which a young child acted as teacher. Because the necessary pedagogic relationship had then to be *made* rather than taken, the child made far more use of intonation and facial expression to convey her meaning, and her instructions were more verbally explicit.(51)

If an observer wishes to reveal the common knowledge underlying classroom interaction, can he treat what is said and what iş left unsaid as evidence of what the participants must be assuming to interact as they do? We return finally to the possibility of reading what is said, not its fine details but its more general characteristics, 'for the sense of the relationship between the speakers that their talk suggests to us'.(52) This possibility is examined at length in the chapters which follow. That it is *worth* examining is suggested by many of the facts about classroom interaction which have been outlined already. Teachers make most of the communicative moves, take most of the initiatives, determine topics and allocate turns. They usually ask questions in which the initiative is retained by the questioner, assessing rather than replying to what pupils say as evidence of participation in their own frame of reference. Certain ways of talking in classrooms can therefore be seen as embodying particular definitions of the situation, while detailed sequences can be interpreted as normal attempts *in that context* to do certain things with words. It is *not* a matter of the context determining what is said, because the process is reciprocal. Teachers and pupils create through talk the very context on which they rely to support that talk. They use their knowledge of the context to generate appropriate behaviour, and the appropriateness of that behaviour then serves to define the context in which they interact. This approach takes account both of situational constraints which authorize certain forms and uses of language, and also of the intricate transmission of social information which takes place during the interaction itself.

In this chapter, we have tried to show how different features of classroom talk are given prominence in different kinds of research, and how different methods of recording and interpreting the facts account for what really occurs. Especially in this final section, we have outlined ideas which largely informed our own research. The brevity of the discussion is justified by its elaboration in later chapters, where these ideas are put to work. In so far as these ideas were worked out *in advance of* classroom observation, then our approach will seem to contradict the ethnographic insistence on presenting a view from the inside. It is the systematic researchers who deliberately distance themselves from those they observe, relying on their special training to reveal what is really taking place. From their perspective, going into classrooms without knowing what to look for would be a waste of time — 'a look-and-see exercise with a catch-what-you-can outcome'.(53) But ethnographic researchers *do* try to catch what they can, making no attempt to control or ignore irrelevant features of the interaction; their account is therefore intended to be *derived from* what happens rather than imposed on it from outside. In practice, however, they cannot avoid beginning their work with some preconceptions about what matters, and these will lead them to pay attention to some incidents and to ignore others. If the researcher then presents the results of his observation as pure description, he is concealing this selectivity. If, on the other hand, he presents his account as being closely guided by theory, then he risks being accused of choosing those events which support his own point of view. Even the most richly detailed case studies are not a preliminary to theorizing about them, because theory will already have determined what kinds of information are being recorded and what questions are asked about that information. Indeed, without some guiding orientation, the observer's attention would wander hopelessly so that he would literally not know which way to look. His account of events would probably be either a fruitless effort to get everything in, or else a haphazard selection of the more dramatic incidents. Since open-mindedness is impossible, what can be demanded of the researcher is that he should make as clear as he can the basis on which he chose to report what he did (since there was so much else going on that he could have noticed), and from which he interpreted his particular collection of facts. If he fails to do this, what is apparently a *description* may seem more convincing than it deserves to be because highly selected observations are so impregnated with interpretation that they can support no other view of reality than the one which is offered. In this chapter, we have outlined the theoretical position from which we entered the field. Chapters 5-7 are, inevitably, a mixture of material illustrating preconceived ideas and of some material which upset those ideas. Some parts of the lessons we recorded fitted our expectations so closely that they could be used to illustrate ideas which we had drawn from the work of others. But there were also times when we had to struggle to make sense of the interaction in ways which seemed to owe little to what others had found in apparently similar situations. Of course, the line between confirmation and discovery is impossible to draw, and any attempt to do so is likely to claim more novelty for the analysis than it deserves. We do claim, however, that our account raises some basic questions about what is normally taken for granted in classroom interaction — questions which have sometimes been asked about classroom management but rarely about the central business of transmitting knowledge.

Chapter 3: Notes and References

1 This approach is exemplified in Medley and Mitzel (1963), 'The Scientific Study of Teacher Behaviour', in Bellack (ed.), *Theory and Research in Teaching*. See also Biddle (1967), 'Methods and Concepts in Classroom Research', *Rev. Educ. Research* 37.

2 Eggleston *et al.* (1976), *Processes and Products of Science Teaching*, p. 24.

3 This argument is elaborated in Furlong and Edwards (1977), 'Language in Classroom Interaction: Theory and Data', *Educ. Research* 19.

4 Amidon and Hunter (1967), *Improving Teaching*, pp. 9–10. The most widely used category systems are described in Amidon and Hough (1967), *Interaction Analysis*; in Gallagher *et al.* (1970), *Classroom Observation*; and in the chapter by Wragg (1975) in Chanan and Delamont (eds), *Frontiers of Classroom Research*.

5 Ober *et al.* (1971), *Systematic Observation of Teaching*, p. 16.

6 The theoretical bases (often implicit) of the main category systems are analysed in Rosenshine and Furst (1973), 'The Use of Direct Observation to Study Teaching', in Travers (ed.), *Second Handbook of Research on Teaching*. Most systems, they suggest, involve 'no more than a description of some aspect of instruction along with an interpretation which objectifies the author's bias' (p. 160).

7 Meacham and Wiesen (1969), *Changing Classroom Behaviour*, p. 11. See also J. Ackerman (1972), *Operant-Conditioning Techniques for the Classroom Teacher*, and Herman (1977), *Creating Learning Environments*.

8 For a systematic study using videotape recording, see Adams and Biddle (1970), *Realities of Teaching*; for an anti-systematic approach which used extensive photographic material, see Walker and Adelman (1972), *Towards a Sociography of Classrooms*.

9 Flanders (1970), *Analysing Teacher Behaviour*, p. 35. An obvious advantage of this method is that 'an hour of observation yields an hour of data' (Rosenshine and Furst, op. cit., p. 149).

10 Ober *et al.* (1971), op. cit., p. 9.

11 The notion of conditional relevance is used to identify sequences of talk in Schegloff (1972), 'Notes on a Conversational Practice', in Sudnow (ed.), *Studies in Social Interaction*, pp. 76–81.

12 Such pseudo-open questions are described in Barnes *et al.* (1969), *Language, the Learner and the School*. These are only apparent by looking beyond the immediate question-answer 'pair', as is clearly recognized in the treatment of teachers' questions by Eggleston *et al.* (1975), *A Science-Teaching Observation Schedule*, p. 8.

13 The democratic ideology underlying a good deal of systematic observation is discussed in Hamilton and Delamont (1974). 'Classroom Research: A Cautionary Tale', *Res. in Educ.* 11: It has never been more overtly expressed than in Anderson's famous paper (1939), 'The Measurement of Dominative and Socially Integrative Behaviour in Teachers' Contacts with Children', *Child Development* 10. In this paper, 'telling' children is assumed to be 'less propitious for growth', and dominative teacher-behaviour is seen as 'the antithesis of the scientific attitude . . . and expression of resistance

against change ... the technique of the dictatorship'. The need for teachers to tighten or relax their instructional direction according to the immediate circumstances is argued by Flanders (1970), op. cit., chapter 10.

14 Amidon and Hunter (1967), op. cit., pp. 3–4. These pragmatic objectives are emphasized by Bealing (1973), 'Issues in Classroom Observational Research', Res. in Educ. 9.

15 The approach is discussed in relation to teacher training by Wragg (1974), Teaching Teaching, pp. 71–102, and applied to the training of teacher trainers by Weller (1971), Verbal Communication in Instructional Supervision. A similar practical appeal has been enjoyed more recently by micro-teaching — see McIntyre et al. (1977), Investigations of Micro-teaching.

16 Smith and Meux (1970), A Study of the Logic of Teaching, provide an extended example of working back from desirable outcomes to the patterns of interaction which preceded them.

17 Flanders (1967), 'Interaction Models of Critical Teaching Behaviour', in Amidon and Hough (eds), op. cit.

18 For an attempt to combine two very different research approaches, see Delamont (1976), 'Beyond Flanders's Fields', in Stubbs and Delamont (eds), Explorations in Classroom Observation.

19 Walker and Adelman (1975a), 'Interaction Analysis in Informal Classrooms', B. J. Ed. Psych. 45; and their chapter 'Strawberries' in Stubbs and Delamont (eds), op. cit.

20 Smith and Geoffrey (1968), Complexities of an Urban Classroom, p. 237.

21 Basic research of this kind is defined in Hymes's introduction (1972) to Cazden et al. (eds), The Functions of Language in the Classroom.

22 The first quotation is from perhaps the earliest definition of a sociological linguistics, a paper by J. R. Firth first published in 1935 and reprinted in Firth (1957), Papers in Linguistics. The second declaration of sociolinguistic interest is from Halliday (1973), Explorations in the Functions of Language, p. 83.

23 Sinclair and Coulthard (1975), Towards an Analysis of Discourse, p. 2.

24 Various settings for talk are compared in this way by Walker and Adelman (1975b), A Guide to Classroom Observation, pp. 84–90.

25 Hymes (1972), 'On Communicative Competence', in Pride and Holmes (eds), Sociolinguistics.

26 Philips (1972), 'Participant-Structures and Communicative Competence', in Cazden et al. (eds), op. cit. Dumont's paper in the same book is overtly political.

27 Halliday (1975), 'Talking One's Way In', in Davies (ed.), Problems of Language and Learning.

28 Blom and Gumperz (1972), 'Social Meaning in Linguistic Structures', in Gumperz and Hymes (eds), Directions in Sociolinguistics.

29 Frender and Lambert (1972), 'Speech Style and Scholastic Success', in Shuy (ed.), Sociolinguistics, p. 245.

30 There is a valuable collection of such studies, including non-verbal communication, in Cazden et al. (1972), op. cit. For a review of sociolinguistic perspectives on classroom register, see Edwards (1976), Language in Culture and Class, pp. 131–42.

31 The social significance of small linguistic differences is brought out in R. Rutherford, 'Talking about Pop', in Rogers (1976), *They Don't Speak Our Language*. Subject languages are discussed in Edwards (1976), op. cit., pp. 150–5 and in Edwards (1978), 'The Language of History', in Dickinson and Lee (eds), *History Teaching and Historical Understanding*.

32 Hymes (1977), *Foundations of Sociolinguistics*, chapter 10.

33 Mishler (1972), 'Implications of Teacher Strategies for Language and Cognition', in Cazden *et al.*, op. cit.

34 Torode (1977), 'Interrupting Inter-Subjectivity', in Woods and Hammersley (eds), *School Experience*.

35 Gumperz and Hymes (eds) (1972), *Directions in Sociolinguistics*, p. 14; Hymes, *Foundations of Sociolinguistics*, pp. 54–5.

36 For an excellent analysis of the inseparability of language from other aspects of social behaviour, see Gumperz (1971), *Language in Social Groups*, chapter 13.

37 Halliday (1973), op. cit., pp. 24 and 51.

38 Barnes (1976), *From Communication to Curriculum*, especially pp. 67–77 and 108–38; Barnes and Todd (1977), *Communication and Learning in Small Groups*, especially chapters 2 and 4.

39 Sinclair and Coulthard (1975), op. cit., p. 6.

40 These common interests are evident in Turner (1970), 'Words, Utterances and Activities', in Douglas (ed.), *Understanding Everyday Life*; and in Wootton (1974), *Dilemmas of Discourse*.

41 Walker and Adelman (1975a), op. cit., p. 74.

42 Such studies are reviewed in Robinson (1974), 'An Ethnography of Classrooms' in Eggleston (ed.), *Contemporary Research in the Sociology of Education*.

43 Furlong (1976), 'Interaction Sets in the Classroom', in Stubbs and Delamont (eds), op. cit., and Furlong (1977), 'Anancy Goes to School', in Woods and Hammersley (eds), op. cit.; Torode (1976), op. cit., and Torode (1977), op. cit.

44 Bernstein (1973), *Class, Codes and Control*, vol. 1, p. 201.

45 For examples of this kind of analysis in non-educational settings, see Wieder (1974), 'Telling the Code', in Turner (ed.), *Ethnomethodology*, and Wootton (1974), op. cit., chapter 1.

46 The speed with which classroom situations change is described, from very different perspectives, by Adams (1971), 'A Sociological Approach to Classroom Research', in Westbury and Bellack (eds), *Research into Classroom Processes*; Hargreaves *et al.* (1975), *Deviance in Classrooms*; Mehan (1974), 'Accomplishing Classroom Lessons', in Cicourel *et al.*, *Language Use and School Performance*; and Sinclair and Coulthard (1975), op. cit.

47 Walker and Adelman (1972), *Towards a Sociography of Classrooms*, p. 27.

48 Cicourel (1973), *Cognitive Sociology*, p. 61.

49 Stebbins (1975), *Teachers and Meaning*, pp. 55–7, 83–4.

50 Hargreaves *et al.* (1975), op cit., pp. 55–6. A similar point is made by Cooper (1976), *Bernstein's Codes: A Classroom Study*, p. 10.

51 Gumperz and Herasimchuk (1972), 'The Conversational Analysis of Social Meaning', in Shuy (ed.), *Sociolinguistics*.

52 Silverman and Jones (1976), *Organizational Work*, p. 19.

53 Ober *et al.* (1971), op. cit., pp. 5–6.

Chapter 4

Contexts for Classroom Talk

Introduction

In this chapter, we provide background information about the school, and about the particular team of teachers who participated in our research. In doing this, we are not merely conforming to a sociological ritual. We are setting out some of the knowledge that we drew on in interpreting the recordings that were made.

Making sense of what is said depends on locating language in the contexts in which it is used. Without considerable knowledge of (for example) the relationship of the speakers and the purposes of their interaction, the words may remain largely mysterious or communicate only the most general meanings. But the knowledge being relied on may be *ir*relevant to that particular context. If we did not provide some detailed background information, readers would still understand the transcripts quoted in the following three chapters through invoking some context of their own. They would have to draw on their knowledge of what *other* schools are like to interpret what was said in this one. Yet Abraham Moss is an unusual school in many ways. During our time there, we came to know something of its organization, and of what the teachers were trying to achieve, and this knowledge underlies our account of the teaching we observed. We now have to ask how much does the reader need to know if he is to follow the sense we made of what was recorded? For it is also important not to present *more* information than was available to us while the analytical work was being done. To do this would risk posing as master-detectives who only discover, or perhaps only reveal, the critical clues on the final pages, and then reinterpret events as though they had known all along what was really going on. Although we chose to work in a community school in an inner-city area, and in a school strongly committed to resource-based learning, we are not presenting a case study in community education, or in curriculum development, or in the schooling of the disadvantaged. We *are* concerned with the kinds of interaction generated in particular classrooms, with how teachers and pupils made sense to each other, and with how an observer can make sense of their doing so. How far an adequate interpretation requires a more *macro*scopic view is something we consider in the final chapter. The presentation of more immediately relevant background information moves in increasing detail from the Centre and its setting to the content and organization of Humanities teaching in the Lower School.(1)

1   The Abraham Moss Centre

The Abraham Moss Centre is a low, white complex of buildings on the borders of Cheetham and Crumpsall, just to the north of the centre of Manchester. Although the site itself was industrial waste ground, it is in the heart of a residential district. A railway runs along one side of it, but in every other direction it is surrounded by semi-detached and terraced housing of the inter-war years. Both Cheetham and Crumpsall were fairly prosperous Victorian developments, but Cheetham in particular has undergone extensive redevelopment. Many of the larger Victorian houses have been taken over for multiple occupation, while large areas of industrial and residential land have been cleared altogether. By the time the clearance programme is completed, almost a quarter of the original housing will have been demolished. By comparison with the city as a whole, it has more than its share of the lower socio-economic groups, of Irish and New Commonwealth immigrants, and of single-parent families.(2) Crumpsall is relatively more stable and more middle class, with much more of its housing dating from the 1920s and 1930s, but here too there are pockets of old and shabby building.

Such areas of urban renewal often lack any clear focus, and the Abraham Moss Centre (which opened in 1973) was planned as a main feature in the rebirth of the community. It houses an eight-form entry comprehensive school, and a college of further education which also provides sixth-form facilities for the school. Altogether, there are now almost 6,000 full-time and part-time students, a staff of well over 200, and a day population of over 3,000. But far more is involved than educational provision of the conventional kind. There is a sports' centre; a district library with a creche adjoining it; a performing-arts centre; a youth club which doubles as a students' union during the day; a club for elderly people; and a small residential wing used largely for students whose parents are ill or otherwise unable to cope with them. All of these come under the direction of the Principal, and are widely used. For example, neither the school nor the college has its own library; both depend on the district library included in the Centre. Similarly, some of the audio-visual and information resources so important to the type of teaching practised in the school are made more generally accessible. In this way, 'whatever is available to the community becomes available to the school, and whatever would normally be available to the school is made available to the community also'.(3)

The thinking behind such an integration of facilities goes back to the work of Henry Morris in the 1920s, and to the Cambridgeshire Village Colleges which were based on his ideas. His notion of a centre for permanent education in the heart of the local community has been echoed in the Crowther, Newsom and Plowden Reports, but the provision at Abraham Moss goes far beyond even that envisaged in the Plowden recommendations. Indeed, it is almost unique in this country both in the extent of the facilities and in the extent to which they have been integrated.(4) In itself, though, this sharing may reflect little more than an attempt at economies of provision. Much more than this is intended at the Centre. The visibility of what it offers is emphasized by the two public rights of way which run through it, and by the siting of several shops alongside the overtly educational buildings. There is therefore a blurring of traditional boundaries between young and old, school and community. Contacts between staff and parents are intended to be easy and informal rather than contained within a framework of institutionalized meetings. But the openness which the Principal hopes to achieve is best exemplified in the plans, still inspirational rather than detailed, for an Open College at which informational and tutorial resources will be available to individuals and groups who wish to study in largely self-directed ways.

Despite their evident novelty, however, the community aspects of the school were not why we chose to work there. Our interest was in the language of teaching, and Abraham Moss was likely to be unusual in that respect too. Resource-based learning with mixed-ability groups has been given a prominence not altogether intended when the Centre was first devised, and this has had a pervasive influence on what language is used to do in the classroom. More generally, it has transformed teaching roles. The teacher is rarely a lone performer. He is committed to a team relationship with colleagues, constrained to collaborate. Much of his professional work is done before he enters the classroom, and the extensive reliance on learning materials demands both expert secretarial and reprographic support and considerable in-service training in this style of teaching. All these services are provided within the Centre.

The philosophy behind this approach to learning, often made explicit by the Principal, is clearly a major influence in recruiting staff.(5) The over-arching concern is with the nature of knowledge in a rapidly changing world, and with the need to train people to 'meet their own needs'. In the school setting, this means avoiding that 'normal' situation in which only the teacher knows how the relevant knowledge is to be doled out and organized so that pupils are necessarily dependent upon him. 'The pupil should not feel that he is fulfilling the teacher's purpose, doing the teacher's work because he has been told to', but should be able to see for himself what that work is and where it is going. The resulting sense of responsibility is seen as of critical importance to both academic and social development. But it is not something to be achieved by exhortation. It requires a long training in how to use sources of information, and a gradually increasing encouragement of self-reliance. Alongside this emphasis on students' organizing their own learning is a clear recognition that inadequate basic skills will limit the autonomy of many of them, and that some forms of learning will need more active and frequent tutorial guidance. But some moves towards independence must begin early. Even in the Lower School, 'while much of the work will involve instruction, help and advice from the teacher . . . the responsibility to learn will be the pupils' '. This is the policy elaborated in the booklet sent out to parents in the summer before their children first enter the school:

> We aim through the Abraham Moss Centre to help our students achieve independence in their learning. In the Lower School, we are aiming to teach them to find out information for themselves and to tackle a carefully constructed programme of work, with the guidance of the teacher but with an increasing amount of independence on the part of the pupil. Gradually, under our supervision and within a well-structured programme, they are able to take more responsibility for their own work and progress, and because they are working for their own intellectual satisfaction, their confidence is increased and their interest in learning is sustained throughout their school career and . . . when they leave the Centre.
> To provide the programmes of work necessary . . . the teachers have worked hard collecting or writing their own materials . . . These programmes involve the use of many new techniques of learning.

A general teaching policy for the entire Centre has therefore been defined with unusual clarity. As we will see, its implementation in the school is reinforced (perhaps even enforced) by geographical and organizational constraints. It was this emphasis on new techniques of learning which attracted us, because of the effects we expected it to have on how language was used in the classroom.

2 The Lower School
Manchester secondary schools are not given special catchment zones.

Parents specify three schools they would like their child to attend, and they normally get one of those choices. Like other schools around it, Abraham Moss therefore has to compete for pupils from the whole of north Manchester, and in the context of a declining school population the competition is real. The intake is seen by the staff as weighted towards the less able child, and there are some obvious reasons for this. In the more middle-class areas within range of the school, there are two older comprehensives which were formerly grammar schools. To draw pupils from those areas, Abraham Moss has to compete on two levels. The rival schools are likely to be seen as better by many parents because of their inherited prestige, while for most middle-class families in the vicinity they were also their most local schools. In recent years too, an increasing number of such families have moved away from the city centre, producing the familiar effect of a population with more than its share of problems. Not surprisingly, then, Abraham Moss is classified as being in an educational priority area, and most of its pupils come from that area. It is not surprising either that the staff are conscious of implementing those new techniques of learning in difficult conditions, conditions which have led elsewhere to some stridently publicized portrayals of chaos and confusion.

This is not the kind of portrait we present in this book. In our many hours of observation, we inevitably saw instances of conflict, as we would have done in any school. What we did *not* see was the persistent state of confrontation between teachers and pupils which seems to characterize many inner-city secondary schools. If the classrooms were sometimes hectic, they were rarely tense. Whatever other advantages resource-based learning may have, it seems to us that breaking up that single verbal encounter which we described in Chapter 2 makes it possible to avoid some otherwise built-in sources of deviance. As we observed it, it also seemed to provide some of the conditions for self-controlled learning. It was because we were impressed by much of the teaching we saw that our initially theoretical concerns came to be more strongly accompanied by the wish to *report* the work being done. This favourable bias was something which largely emerged *during* the research. Our original choice of school had been objective in so far as we wanted to observe innovative classrooms in a secondary school, and there seemed to be few of these within easy reach. We began work there favourably disposed to what was being attempted, but not very optimistic that we would find it being done. Furlong had previously taught in a London comprehensive where the only orderly classrooms were traditional in organization. Edwards had taught mainly in grammar schools, but had visited many comprehensives in different parts of the country; few had seemed chaotic, but even fewer to be making any significant break from the transmission model of teaching. Our initial expectations of Abraham Moss were therefore that things would either be *not* very different, or different but confused. We were pleased to find that we were wrong — that there *were* differences *without* much apparent confusion.

To avoid some of the organizational confusion which might otherwise occur in so large and complex an establishment, the Centre is broken down into small, interdependent units. The Lower School has 480 children aged 11 – 13. Physically, it is almost self-contained. Organizationally too, it has considerable autonomy. It has its own head teacher, and while the premises are used for other purposes out of hours, daytime timetabling is restricted to its own pupils. The thinking behind this separation is that the school should provide an easily identifiable base in which children can feel at home. From its comparative security, they can then be involved gradually in the life of the Centre as a whole.

The buildings of the Lower School consist of four areas, or suites of rooms, which are on two floors around a central courtyard. Four teams of teachers work within these areas, the curriculum being integrated under the labels Art and Craft, Communications and Modern Languages, Humanities, and Science and Mathematics. Each curriculum territory is large enough to accommodate 120 children at a time, so that half of each year can be timetabled together. Each contains classrooms of normal size, an open area, and various specialized facilities. Close collaboration between teachers is therefore unavoidable. Unmistakable messages are communicated by these contexts 'from their makers to their users'. Indeed, the design of the whole Centre, 'firmly based on the observed practice of first-class teachers', is described by one of its 'makers' as explicitly intended to replace 'the authoritarian posture of the lonely performer' by more co-operative forms of teaching.[6] The resulting physical constraints are reinforced by ideological and organizational pressures against teachers' traditional freedom to devise their own materials and ways of working. This autonomy is seen by the Principal as being at best wasteful, and at worst the 'pedagogical arrogance' of those who think that *they* have nothing to learn. It is also associated with sharply defined subject boundaries. The teaching teams which cover the entire curriculum of the Lower School are intended to combine the various skills of their members, and to provide a source of mutual training in the use of new techniques. As in the extensive use of curriculum packages (freely adapted to local conditions), they are an attempt to get away from that 'arrogant' self-sufficiency which leads so many teachers to proceed as though they had nothing to learn or inherit from other skilled practitioners.[7] Bernstein has argued that such integrated approaches depend on 'high ideological consensus among the staff' if they are to be more than superficial and piecemeal. We do not want to exaggerate either the extent or the explicitness of consensus, and no doubt there are conflicts in the school over how common commitments to (for example) mixed-ability teaching, self-regulated learning, and close collegial relationships between staff, are to be interpreted and implemented.(8) But alongside the ideological support for moves in these directions, there is the kind of organizational support best exemplified by looking closely at one of the curriculum areas.

3   Lower-School Humanities

As in many schools, Humanities is not an addition to the traditional diet of separate subjects, but a radical departure from 'pure' categories of knowledge. It replaces history, geography, religious education, and some aspects of English. To see that the skills supposedly developed by these disciplines are not being neglected, there are specialist consultants who hold a watching brief for their subjects throughout the Centre. Though the status is much the same, the title of head of department is avoided so as not to reflect old knowledge boundaries too strongly in the teaching hierarchy. Consultants have some control over the allocation of resources, are available for advice, and sometimes participate in team discussions. But the day-to-day work of the team is left to the teachers themselves, under the guidance of a co-ordinator. Again, the avoidance of the title of leader is deliberate.

Successful departures from the more familiar 'vertical' chain of command depend on the team members' interacting often enough to confirm (or modify) common procedures.(9) The cohesiveness of the team we observed was a striking feature of their work. Organizational conditions made this cohesion possible. For example, four of the five teachers taught nothing but Lower-School Humanities during that school year. Some collaboration was forced on the team by the inclusion in their territory of an open area in which they worked in pairs. Further collaboration was *encouraged* by the provision of a small office to act as a headquarters, and by timetabling the equivalent of a double period each week for a planning meeting at which to discuss problems and keep up to date on pupils' progress. Notes were taken so that absent members could be kept informed of decisions and there was a record to appeal to in case of dispute. There were also short routine meetings before the beginning of each school day, and a great deal of informal and out-of-hours discussion. Such organizational backing is a necessary, but not of course a sufficient, cause of cohesion.(10) The commitment of these particular teachers to working together was reflected in the frequency and intensity of their informal discussions, and in their decision to continue their collaboration in the following school year. Yet the team was a new one. Only one of the teachers had taught Lower-School Humanities from the start in 1973; he was also assistant head of the second year, with many pastoral responsibilities. The co-ordinator was in his third year at the school, but his previous teaching had been mainly with older children. The two other full-time team members were both new to the school; one had previously taught in primary schools, and the other was in her probationary year. The fifth teacher taught half-time in the team, and was also Director of Resources for the whole Centre (he has since been made an Assistant Principal). Taken together, then, the team represented a blend of experience, inexperience, and differing experience. Their interdependence in almost every aspect of their teaching made possible some pooling of their various skills, and provided support for the two new teachers which both of them readily acknowledged. It also made many common practices inevitable, whatever reservations individuals might feel about some of them. But at least in terms of broad strategy, they seemed in close agreement. As one of them put it, the Principal had given the school its emphasis on resouce-based learning, and his ideas had attracted staff interested in that way of teaching. Both collectively and individually, the team tended to use a vocabulary of pupil responsibility, of learning how to learn, and of the teacher's deliberate retreat from being the main source of authoritative information.

The content of the Humanities course has been the object of continuing reappraisal since the school began. Much of the material we saw in use had been revised by, and then inherited from, past members of the team. Some of it was revised immediately before, or during, the year we were at the school. What might be called collective critical introspection is a frequent justification of team teaching, and it would be quite arbitrary to try to disentangle current innovations from the residues of past structurings and restructurings. First-year work had originally been based on themes from the Keele Integrated Studies Project, though its origins were largely lost to view in the many changes made since. It was concerned with how human life first began, how nomadic groups began to live in settled communities, and how people began to make sense of their world through their myths and their gods. Particular communities were studied in detail so as to show different ways of adapting to the physical environment, and the year ended with a project on the history and present-day life of Cheetham and Crumpsall. The second-year work was based on 'Man: A Course of Study', though again in a form considerably adapted from the original. MACOS is an American discovery-based curriculum, devised under the supervision of the psychologist Jerome Bruner and representing a striking example of an explicit theory of *instruction* being put to work. It was an attempt to provide children aged 9—13 with a set of concepts for thinking about the deep structure of human experience. In three comparatively simple animal studies, pupils are introduced to certain basic conceptual tools — for example, to ideas of innate and learned behaviour, adaptation and natural selection, structure and function, information and communication. This work leads up to Bruner's central question, 'What is human about being human?', and to study of the five great humanizing forces of tool-making, child-rearing, socialization, language, and the urge to explain the world. A half-year course on the preliterate Netsilik Eskimo community is organized around these five forces.(11)

It is obviously impossible to do justice to these projects in a marginal note. But we have to refer briefly to the originals, and then in rather more detail to their adaptation in the teaching we observed. Both courses emphasize the systematic development of key concepts through detailed study of the unfamiliar, descriptions of human and animal behaviour being used to raise questions about coping with environmental problems which in turn raise general questions about the human condition. How far children can be said to be discovering is an intriguing question, since the concepts are clearly there to be found and the case studies lead thought in the required directions. Both courses leave plenty of scope for teacher exposition too, though there are also banks of supplementary information which pupils can use for themselves. At Abraham Moss, much of this material has been both rewritten and extended. Indeed, one benefit of team teaching has been the occasional opportunity to free a teacher to concentrate on such revisions. For example, both standard and easier booklets have been produced, covering the same facts and concepts but accessible to different levels of reading competence. Pupils were usually allowed to choose their own level, though the teacher might decide for them if they seemed to be either coasting along or persisting with a text beyond their current skills. For some parts of the courses, there were also readers available for those who found the main booklets especially difficult. These introduced key words and concepts essential to the text, and then used a tape-recording to guide the pupil through a simplified version of it.

Widespread use of already packaged materials may easily attach pupils and teachers to an informational conveyor-belt. But even more than in the courses on which Humanities teaching had originally been based, the central core of information was surrounded by other material (reference books, tapes, films, and films which pupils could show for themselves on simple cassette projectors) to which the basic tasks could lead or to which children could turn on their own initiative. This diversity of resources was apparent in the layout of the teaching rooms, and it both reflected and made possible a sharp reduction in teacher performances of the traditional kind.

4 Inside the Classroom

Normally, the teaching of each half-year (120 children) took place simultaneously in the two classrooms and the open area. There was also a small tutorial room which could be used for individual work, especially when slow readers were using a tape-recorder, and a library room housing general encyclopedias and a selection of books about the topics being studied at the time. A hall, shared with Art and Craft, was used when all 120 children needed to be together for a film or a lead lesson.

Neither the classrooms nor the open area were organized on traditional lines. There was no grid of desks, no dais, and no channelling of communication to and from the front of the room. Pupils worked individually, or in groups of two or three, at tables spaced irregularly around the room, and the most physically obvious focus of their activities was not the teacher's desk but the resources trolley in the centre of the room. This trolley contained all the booklets that different groups were currently using, and was replenished as the topic changed. The walls were covered with pictures and charts, often produced by the children themselves. In the autumn term, a large mural was made by first-year pupils showing the development of life from the early sea creatures to man, while displays appeared later on the life of the Netsilik and on the religious beliefs of different peoples of the world. Because of the care taken with these displays, and the organization of teaching space, the rooms seemed more like the upper classes of a primary school than the more formal and visually barren settings so often associated with secondary education.

We referred earlier to the messages communicated by physical settings. These messages must not be made to look too imperious, as though the users' options were thereby removed. As we will see in Chapter 7, the teachers felt some doubts about what the basic layout of the rooms both symbolized and reinforced — the deflection of attention away from themselves as the main source of authoritative information. The arrangement and uses of the open area had evolved considerably over a period of four years, and there were marked differences in the appearance of the two classrooms, especially in the extent to which communication was spatially decentralized. The more experienced members of the team said they felt more relaxed in the classrooms, where the greater physical closure reduced the number of distractions and provided a sense of structure which they thought many children welcomed. Not surprisingly, the two new teachers felt less isolated in the open area and enjoyed 'the security of having another teacher there'. With one exception, however, styles of teaching did not seem to us to vary much between the two settings. The exception was a rough (though informal) division of labour between whichever of the teachers were working together in the open area. One took on the managerial role of 'shouter', while the other concentrated on the problems of individual pupils. Though the label is the team's own, we emphasize that the shouter did not often have to shout. The role was more supervisory than disciplinary. While it might be exchanged during the course of a single lesson, it was seldom that two teachers shouted together.

There were six thirty-five-minute periods of Humanities each week. Groups of thirty pupils were assigned to one teacher, who had primary responsibility for their progress throughout the year. Whether they were in a classroom or in the open area, the normal pattern was the same: they were to collect the appropriate booklet promptly and get down to work. Achieving this routine with new pupils involved the teachers in a great deal of effort, but once established it left more and more time for dealing with individual queries and difficulties. We have seen how a trained capacity for independent work is the main long-term objective at the Centre, and how the groundwork for such independence is supposed to be done in the Lower School. The initiation of first-year children into making unsupervised use of various sources of information was a main preoccupation of the teachers, partly because most local primary schools were thought to have given little preparation for it, and partly because their expectations of secondary school teachers were seen as being derived from a stereotype of someone 'standing up there and spouting'. There were bound to be some, therefore, who found it confusing 'not to be talked down to and not to be treated as a class and told what to do', and many more who needed a long apprenticeship before they could learn in other ways than by 'responding to authority in the front of the class'.(12)

The use of clearly structured course materials helped to develop independent learning, in so far as children could see for themselves the larger programme into which their immediate tasks fitted. But reliance on such materials also brought to the surface anxieties about the resulting transformation in the teacher's role, anxieties which we consider more closely in Chapter 7. Briefly, traditional charismatic teaching was seen as an attack on pupil autonomy, at least when it was more than an occasional performance, and its renunciation had required considerable powers of self-control. Indeed, recalling his experience in firmly traditional classrooms, Edwards was struck by the superficial resemblence of one lesson to the next, and by the limited scope for conventional displays of the teachers' erudition and wit. Whatever the advantages for pupils, things seemed to be more monotonous *for the teachers*.(13) As we will see, this apparent monotony concealed very varied forms of troubleshooting, in which there was time for the diagnosis and treatment of pupils' difficulties to be more carefully considered than is normally the case with whole-class teaching. Nevertheless, the infrequency of activities involving whole groups of children together had begun to worry the teachers themselves. Occasional bursts of teacher exposition seemed to be resented by children as an interruption of their own working schedule, and while this might seem to exemplify the triumph of self-directed learning, it could also imply an undervaluing of the teacher, who had more to offer than being 'an adjunct of the booklets'. As one of them remarked, 'It's that we are no longer resources of information, we're resources of where to find information'.

The traditional starring role, then, had largely disappeared. The usual structure of Humanities lessons involved the pupils in working through the booklets, and the teachers in trouble-shooting rather than in telling. The revelation of trouble was largely on the pupil's initiative. Children who were stuck would either put up their hands or walk out to wherever the teacher was located. Occasionally, a teacher would ask certain pupils to bring out their work for scrutiny, and there was undoubtedly both a rough rota system which guaranteed each child some attention and a priority system for keeping some children's work more persistently in view. But there were many lessons too which brought a steady stream of immediate difficulties with which the teacher had to cope. Although the strain of managing a central communication system was usually absent, the transformed teaching role was certainly no less exhausting. The following record of part of one lesson is untypical in the frequency of very short encounters, but it indicates how pressing could be the demands on scarce resources of teachers' time and energy.(14) Because of late arrivals, and some tardiness in getting down to work, this group had taken a fair time to settle. While they did so, the teacher stayed in one position near the door, dealing with perhaps a dozen individuals as they entered:

> (11.12 a.m.) The teacher goes over to two boys who seem unable to start work, and a third boy follows him. (11.13) Two other boys arrive to seek help. (11.15) The teacher moves to a table where three girls are working.

While he deals with them, another girl stands behind him waiting for his attention; as he finishes talking to her, a boy asks for a new exercise book. (11.16) While the teacher is away fetching the book, there is no obvious increase in noise. (11.19) He stands by a group of four boys, giving most of his attention to one of them and then moving around the others. (11.23) He is summoned by a girl on the other side of the room, talks to her briefly, then stands watching as she returns to her work. (11.25) Two girls approach him for help. As they go away, his attention is required by the boy sitting nearest him; the ensuing conversation is interrupted twice by queries from other pupils, and once by a rebuke to someone for wasting time. (11.28) The teacher moves towards a girl with her hand up, but his progress is halted by a question from the opposite side of the room. This is answered, but the still puzzled questioner tries to resume contact. The teacher gives priority to the girl who is still waiting. (11.30) Some time is spent with a boy who has 'done nothing', and in checking on two girls who also seem to be taking time off. (11.34) The teacher goes over to the previous puzzled questioner, and talks to him through three querying interruptions.

We emphasize again that encounters with individuals and small groups were usually more prolonged than this, but the record indicates the main pattern of teacher activity.

There were also occasional lead lessons, especially with the first-year children. Both courses are organized into units or themes, and new topics were often introduced in this way so that everyone could move on at the same time. This lock-step method brings obvious problems, because there will be large differences in the ground children have covered. These difficulties of pacing the work were partly overcome by using several levels of booklet, and by setting additional tasks for those who finished early. The right time for introducing a new topic was decided at the planning meetings, where the team might agree to extend work that had proved interesting or cut short something that had failed to arouse much enthusiasm. They certainly seemed to have avoided that deference to course material that brings the pressures of inexorable deadlines.(15).

5   Notes on Observation and Data

At the end of the previous chapter, we set out the theoretical guidelines of our research. After the necessary interlude of setting the scene, we now turn to some of their practical implications.

If we were to see how shared meanings were built up and maintained through classroom talk, it was necessary to get to know a few classrooms well. We also expected that when children entered a new environment, a great deal of what would later be taken for granted would have to be talked about in some detail. We therefore chose to concentrate on first-year pupils so that we could record their introduction to new ways of working, together with some examples of how they worked later in the year when these procedures had been established. There have been very few studies of settling in, largely because researchers are reluctant to intrude on the early encounters of teacher and pupils. Yet the meanings being exchanged then may be unusually accessible to the researcher, who will be close to the participants' own state of knowledge.(16)

Before we began either observation or recording, we sent a statement of intent to the teachers with whom we would be working, and to other staff at the Centre who might be interested in, or wary of, what we planned to do. Though our aims inevitably exceeded our grasp, the following extracts set out what we thought we were doing at the outset of the research:

> We begin by assuming that Abraham Moss teachers are trying to move away from traditional teacher-pupil relationships to establish new *ways of working* as well as new forms of curriculum content.What we hope to explore is how teachers use talk to define with their pupils what school-work is, and what the learner's role is to be. For example, what kind of response does a teacher want when he asks a question? Is he implicitly asking for a repetition of information already provided, or does he intend pupils to explore different approaches to the question? . . .
>
> When a new group of pupils enters the school, we assume that teachers will have to devote some time to 'grooving them in' to the new ways of working. They will have to be more explicit than usual about what they mean when they ask questions, give instructions, or evaluate answers. By making recordings during the first few weeks of the school year, we hope that it will be possible to identify both the explicit guide-lines *and* what pupils and teachers seem to be taking for granted about their relationships . . . We also hope to make a number of follow-up recordings at different times during the year, as well as some with second-year groups where the contrasts with traditional classrooms may be more apparent.
>
> Some further points need to be made about what we will *not* be doing. We are only interested in normal classroom activities, and it is therefore in our interest (as well as the school's!) to disrupt lessons as little as possible. We are in no way concerned with evaluating either teachers or pupils. We have no experiments to carry out, and no clearly defined hypotheses to test. We *are* interested in discovering what kind of talk goes on in open classrooms, and how this talk can be described . . .
>
> Though traditional and open are obviously vague labels, they refer not only to the authoritarian nature of teacher-pupil relationships but to the kind of meanings exchanged between them. Accounts of social class differences in language often assume that the range of uses to which language is put in classrooms is too wide for many pupils. There is some evidence now that it is too *restricted* — that classroom knowledge is pre-

sented as something to be taken rather than made, and that the communicative initiative is usually retained by the teacher. In open classrooms, pupils are likely to have more sense of control over the learning problems facing them . . . Though it is a hunch we would not want to dignify as a hypothesis, we feel that their classroom language is likely to show a wider functional range than that apparent in traditional classrooms. Part of our task will be to see if this can be recognized in what they say.

We started our pursuit of this hunch by making our first visits to the school in the summer of 1976. Observation and recording began in the first weeks of the autumn term. After close study of the transcripts, and much rethinking of our problems, we returned for a further period of recording in February 1977. The interaction of observation, recording, and analysis continued into the summer term, when the final recordings were made. Twenty-eight lessons were recorded altogether, all of them involving the three men in the Humanities team. No sexist bias should be inferred from this. Both women teachers were new to the school, and one was new to teaching. With so much settling in to do themselves, it seemed unfair to subject them to the additional tensions and inconvenience of being recorded. But both were observed teaching, and while there were certainly differences in teaching style between all members of the team, they did not seem to differ in basic strategies.

Because we wanted detailed transcripts from settings where the teachers were unusually mobile, we used a radio-microphone which the teacher wore around his neck, and a small receiver which picked up what was said to him and by him in any part of the room. As a supplement to the recording, the observer wrote down what was happening while the talk was going on. This commentary was inevitably both partial and superficial. Walker and Adelman described the informal classrooms they observed as being so unusual that they could not have made sense of the verbal interaction without the full film record which they made.(17) We had no access to the kinds of equipment they used, but we did not feel the bewilderment they might have predicted. This was perhaps because we concentrated mainly on first-year teaching, which was organized in more verbally explicit ways. If we had chosen to work more with the MACOS-based curriculum, where the children were often using several quite different resources in the same lesson, then we too might have found the words alone incomprehensible. Nevertheless, technical limitations obviously influenced the direction our analysis has taken. We had to look almost entirely at the more *verbal* encounters between teachers and pupils. We also had to abandon our original intention of recording pupil-pupil talk, because doing so with our meagre technical resources produced recordings so frequently inaudible that the only remedy would have been to withdraw small groups from their normal setting. Apart from the resulting disruption of lessons, this practice would have been irrelevant to our purpose of studying varieties of talk *ordinarily* generated by resource-based learning.(18) But we were therefore forced to concentrate far more heavily on teacher-talk than we had planned to do. Although we talked to individual pupils about particular activities, and about their understanding of certain sections of their course, the main form of checking back was to show transcripts and interpretations to the teachers concerned, and invite their comments on what we thought had been going on. On a more general level, two drafts of the book have been seen by the five teachers we observed, by past members of the Humanities team, by the Head of Lower School, and by the Principal of the Centre. Our account has benefited greatly from their response.

Recognition of these benefits reminds us of a question which we raised in the introduction, and to which we return in the final chapter. What is the relationship between what the researcher sees, and the participants' view of those events? Putting the point crudely, should talking about teaching be a collaborative activity, or is the researcher specially equipped to do the talking? For the moment, we take up only two points of immediate relevance. When we were planning our research, we intended to ask pupils and teachers how they interpreted what had recently been said between them. In practice, this proved too disruptive. But we came to doubt the value of doing so for reasons which arise from quite basic features of classroom life — the complexity and fluidity which have already been described. 'It seems that the teacher has partly, or even completely defined the ongoing situation, but is unable to act before the scene has changed so significantly that a new plan of action is called for.'(19) To recollect in tranquillity is to describe a *different* situation, because the narrator now knows what happened next. Retrospection by teachers or pupils may well slide over the many improvizations which occurred, and so present an unrealistically tidy and consistent version of the facts. It was only by basing his analysis of how teachers evaluate pupils' performance on detailed study of transcripts that Hugh Mehan was able to show 'how the child's contextually situated understanding of instruction and the teacher's interpretation of the child's performance is accomplished anew each time questions are asked and answers are given'. The knowledge underlying their interaction might indeed be reported quite fully in the abstract, but it has to be put to use in actual situations which may make necessary all kinds of modification. Only close study of transcripts could therefore begin to capture 'the innovation and emergence found in classroom interaction'.(20)

Mehan's emphasis on transcript evidence for what was going on led him to present enough of it for the reader to be able to make up his own mind about the interpretation being offered. While we have adopted this practice ourselves, it may seem more convincing than it deserves. Detailed examples may indeed give the reader some feel for the interaction being described, and they are preferable to a coding of the original observations which leaves the reader entirely dependent on the researcher's version of events. But even the fullest display of evidence is still highly selective. It may be intended to allow the reader to decide for himself whether things really look that way, but the researcher has the benefit of much greater background knowledge which allows him to fill out very persuasively the meaning of what happened. Even when the transcript of an entire lesson precedes any analysis of it, that analysis is still likely to transform the reader's preliminary sense of what occurred.(21) It is much more likely, however, that the presentation will be of edited highlights. If the editing is sufficiently ruthless, it is unlikely to support any other version of the facts than the one being offered.(22) We have tried ourselves to make the basis of our account as explicit as possible, to indicate some of the ways in which our ideas changed as we studied the transcripts, and to present many examples so as to show what we took from them. If these examples were not consciously chosen for their confirming power, we have to recognize that they undoubtedly fit the exposition developed in the three chapters which follow.

Chapter 4: Notes and References

1   Much of this background information we owe to conversations with the team of teachers we observed, and with the Head of Lower School. We also read several published accounts of the Centre's work, and are grateful to its Principal for the opportunity to consult some unpublished papers.

2

	Cheetham	Manchester
% social 'classes' 4 & 5	42.3	31.3
% immigrants (Irish, New Commonwealth and Foreign)	24.0	9.6
% single-parent families	27.2	14.9
		(1971 Census)

3   Mitson and Holder (1974), 'Comprehensive Education within a Community Centre', *Forum* 16, p. 90.
4   Hall (1975), 'Forging Links with a Social System', *Education* 21.
5   Mitson (1974), 'With Community in Mind', *Secondary Education* 4.3; Mitson and Holder (1974), op. cit.; Mitson (1977), 'Resources not for Resources' Sake', in Jennings (ed.), *Management and Headship in the Secondary School*.
6   Some of the messages intended by the planners of the Abraham Moss

Centre are set out in the article by Jackson Hall (1975), op. cit. Hall was Deputy Education Officer for Manchester at that time.

7 Team teaching is justified in similar ways in Worrall *et al.* (1970), *Teaching from Strength*. The Principal of Abraham Moss was one of the writers of this book.

8 The organization of the Lower School seems to be a relatively pure example of the integrated type described by Bernstein (1971), 'On the Classification and Framing of Educational Knowledge', in Young (ed.), *Knowledge and Control*. For attempts to apply Bernstein's typology to particular comprehensive schools, see Hamilton (1973), 'The Integration of Knowledge', *J. Curr. Studies* 5; and Hanan (1975), 'The Problem of the Unmotivated Pupil in an Open School', in Chanan and Delamont (eds), *Frontiers of Classroom Research*.

9 Vertically (leader) and horizontally (colleague) controlled teaching teams are described in Martin (1975), 'The Negotiated Order of Teachers in Team-Teaching Situations', *Soc. Educ.* 48.

10 The absence of some necessary conditions is apparent in Hamilton's accounts of integrated science-teaching in a school where the scheme was taught by too many different teachers who were rarely in contact with one another, were still mainly committed to subject teaching higher up the school, and who lacked the resources to move far from transmission teaching. See Hamilton (1973), op. cit., and Hamilton (1975), 'Handling Innovation in the Classroom', in Reid and Walker, *Case Studies in Curriculum Change*.

11 The Keele Project is described in the Schools Council (1972) publication, *Exploration Man*. The theory on which MACOS is based is clearly stated in chapter 4 of Bruner (1966), *Toward a Theory of Instruction*, and translated in the Course Guides into very specific guidance for teachers using it.

12 Quoted comments are taken from our recorded discussions with the team.

13 The difficulty experienced by teachers in taking the back seat required in the Nuffield Humanities Project is described in Stenhouse (1973), 'The Humanities Project', in Butcher and Pont (eds), *Educational Research in Britain* 3.

14 The pressures in more conventional classrooms are vividly described in Jackson (1968), *Life in Classrooms*; in Jackson and Lahaderne (1967), 'Inequalities of Teacher–Pupil Contacts', *Psychology in the Schools* 4; and in Hilsun and Cane (1971), *The Teacher's Day*.

15 Missing completion dates was a main preoccupation in the team teaching meetings described by Hamilton, op. cit.

16 Delamont (1976), *Interaction in the Classroom*, p. 90.

17 Walker and Adelman (1972), *Towards a Sociography of Classrooms*.

18 The reasons why Barnes and Todd (1977) withdrew children from the classroom to record their talk were also partly technical. From their perspective, the further justification is entirely valid, namely, that placing them in a demanding situation eliciting optimum performance was valuable in showing teachers who are so often reluctant to let groups of pupils talk on their own what could be achieved without the authoritative presence of the teacher. See Barnes and Todd, *Communication and Learning in Small Groups*.

We echo their comments on the tedious and time-consuming task of making transcripts.

19   Stebbins (1975), *Teachers and Meaning*, pp. 91–4. Stebbins stresses the point made in our Introduction — the immediacy of classroom events and the frequent need for teachers to react without reflection.

20   Mehan (1974), 'Accomplishing Classroom Lessons', in Cicourel *et al.*, *Language Use and School Performance*, p. 113. Mehan describes a teacher's surprise at discovering that she had *not* applied consistently her rules for evaluating children's answers.

21   Hammersley (1977), 'School Learning', in Woods and Hammersley (eds), *School Experience*. But Hammersley is properly explicit that the evidence he presents does not constitute a test of his account of it.

22   In Torode (1976), 'Teacher's Talk and Classroom Discipline', in Stubbs and Delamont (eds), *Explorations in Classroom Observation*, six months' observation is distilled into a few lines of transcript, which then support an analysis which has to be taken on trust because so little is said about how it was derived from the full record.

Chapter 5

Settling In

Introduction

The guiding perspective in our interpretation of classroom talk is that much of what is being talked about is not put into words. Yet the participants need evidence that they are making sense to one another. Since talk is the main source of such reassurance, *what* needs to be said and *how much* needs to be said? What kinds of verbal information do teachers and pupils need to receive and to transmit in order to sustain their classroom identities? What must they be taking for granted to leave certain things unsaid? These questions are usefully asked first about the interaction of teachers and pupils newly confronting one another, because in these early encounters it may be easier to observe the relevant relationships being talked into existence.

The interaction which we interpret in this chapter involved pupils in their first weeks in the school. Most of it was recorded in the first four full Humanities lessons. The children were new to the school, to the teachers, and to the study of Humanities. However indirect the teachers intended their influence to be later in the year, they had to be explicit about those procedures on which later lessons would depend. They had to talk appropriate definitions of the situation into existence, maintain and reinforce them, and remove any ambiguities. But the children were *not* new to school, to teachers, or to systematically organized 'school knowledge'. For all their surface differences, classrooms are similar in many of their communicative (and other) requirements. Confronting a new class of eleven-year-olds, a teacher can therefore rely on many ready-made clues to what he means — or at least he is likely to do so until he receives some indications that these do not exist. He assumes some reciprocity of perspectives because he assumes that his pupils already know in general terms what classrooms are like, and what are the normal limits of proper pupil-behaviour. Of course they also have a large stock of more general knowledge on which he implicitly relies. An obvious item is the possession of a common language, and the second lesson provided a vivid example of this basic assumption being contradicted:

5.1   P: Sir, she hasn't got a book 'cos she weren't here last week.
     T: Oh, are you new? Oh, why didn't you tell me?
     P: Sir, she doesn't speak English.
     T: Doesn't speak English. Ah.
     P: She understands some things but . . .
     T: Yeah, right, well, we'll have to get you a book, then, anyway. Has Mr ——— talked to you?
     P: ((Silence.))
     T: Where are you from?
     P: ((whispers)) Persia.
          Ah! Um, are you going to be here all year? ((Silence; teacher talks more slowly.)) Will you be at this school all year?
     P: ((Silence.))
     T: How can I say that in any other way? ((Very slowly.)) How long will you be here? ((Silence.)) Oh, sorry — um, how long have you been in England?
     P: I have for, um, for twenty-five or twenty-six days.
     T: Twenty-six days — oh, is that all? Uh, and how long *will you* be in England? How long will you stay in England?
     P: Studying English.
     T: For how long? ((The teacher spent a considerable time with the girl, making sure that she knew his name and the group that she was in, and that she could read at least a little English.))(1)

Although such fundamental contradictions are not uncommon in classrooms, this chapter is concerned with more narrowly situational knowledge. To use a now unfashionable term, teachers and pupils were entering into a *role* relationship. In Bernstein's definition which we quoted earlier, roles involve 'a constellation of learned shared meanings which enables an individual to enter into persistent, consistent and recognized forms of interaction with others'; these meanings cannot be understood apart from the relevant context, and the context 'cannot be read by those who do not share the history of the relationship'.(2) Now the *particular* relationships we were observing in these classrooms had no history. They were in the first stages of being constructed. But in so far as they constituted a *type* of relationship, then teachers and pupils were able to rely on what they already knew about the 'consistent forms of interaction involved'. They could use that background knowledge to clarify ambiguities, fill in the gaps in what was said, and avoid spelling out 'what everybody knows'. As we recorded and analysed these early lessons, we were interested in what was being taken for granted and what *was* being spelled out.

1 Establishing Procedural Competence

We begin our account with some mundane procedural examples because that is where the teachers themselves began. They had decided to make the detailed organization of Humanities lessons as clear as possible so as to avoid the confusion which had sometimes arisen in previous years from trying to change too much too quickly. In spelling out these details, they assumed that the children already knew enough to be going on with about *general* classroom behaviour. This assumption was largely justified in so far as pupils rarely misbehaved. The teachers could therefore get on with the job of building up more specific forms of appropriate behaviour — of progressively defining what competent interaction was to be in those classrooms in that area of the curriculum. Some of what pupils already knew about classroom procedures could be allowed to stand; at least for the time being, it was still relevant. But where things were going to be different, or where general rules were to apply in particular ways, then details had to be made explicit which could later be taken as read. At the simplest procedural level, for example, the activity of packing up was very fully described so that pupils would later be able to fill in the relevant meanings for themselves. This is the process which Smith and Geoffrey described as grooving in. Administrative, disciplinary, and instructional rules are announced, refined, and repeated so that pupils come to accept certain ways of doing things as normal in that context. As the process continues, the rules largely sink out of sight. Explicit descriptions become implicit prescriptions, and teachers can refer more and more obliquely to how things are (and ought to be) done.(3) A great deal is said in the early stages of the interaction so that little or nothing needs to be said later. A procedural map is being drawn, the salient features of which will later be taken for granted.

We group some examples of this procedural settling in under three broad headings. If the examples seem mundane, they nevertheless represent those matters that were most prominent in the teachers' early talk. They also lead the analysis back to what was mainly being taken for granted — the underlying structure of the classroom relationships.

(a) Getting down to work

First lessons are always difficult. In Abraham Moss, some normal difficulties were intensified. The children came from a large number of primary schools, so that they were usually strangers to one another. The unfamiliar label for this part of their timetable meant that past experience of history or geography was not obviously of much use, and there were no ready-made frames of reference such as the traditional school subjects provide. In the particular lessons we observed, sixty pupils were gathered together in an open area too confined to allow much scope for confusion. In these conditions, organizational matters took precedence. The children had to learn to come in quickly, find their places, get the materials necessary for work, and appear busy. All these activities can be summarized as 'getting down to work'.

Classrooms are about work. They are places of purposeful activity, even when the purposes of the actual activity taking place are not at all clear. That pupils should appear to be busy most of the time is a general rule that only needs to be recalled and reinforced, rather than constructed anew with each group of pupils.(4) Of course, knowledge of the *particular* forms of work required, of what it means to be appropriately busy in that part of the curriculum, is not something that can be taken for granted. But in these first lessons, what was done was less important than that *something* should be done. With so many children likely to be bothered and bewildered, the teachers had to free themselves to deal with the problems of individuals. The best way to do this was to give the less bewildered something to keep them occupied which looked like school-work. We 'knew' this from our own teaching experience, and our 'knowledge' was confirmed in conversation with the teachers themselves. Other reasons were made obvious in what was actually said at the time. For example, *at least* two things were being done in the following sequences (the 'at least' reminds us that beneath the surface of the interaction, the basic authority of the teacher was being announced and reinforced). Particular procedures were being established which would persist throughout the year, and an emphasis on self-directed learning was already being introduced. That this *was* what was happening in these early lessons was made explicit at several points:

5.2   T: OK, we'll do that, then. In future, when you come into this lesson, you come in, you put your bag on the floor by your place and then quickly go and get a booklet yourself, and you'll find that it works. You might think that there'll be sixty kids all charging over there at the same time, but it doesn't happen. You'll find that you'll be able to come in, walk quietly over to the trolley, get the booklet that you need, go back to your place, and you'll be ready to start work : : : : Are *you* listening?

P: ((Nods.))

T: What are we going to do with your books?

P: Sir, you'll put them down on the trolley.

T: Right. You'll find your books on that trolley. ((Further elaboration and repetition of the instructions.)) And we'll see if that works. You'll be able to come in, get your book, go and collect your booklet, sit down and get down to work. In that way, we don't have to spend ten minutes while you have to wait for everything to be done — while you have to wait for us to start you off. You'll be able to get yourself going all on your own.

In the following lesson, when many of the children were late arriving in the open area, one of the teachers commented to the other as they awaited the stragglers, 'I wonder if we'll need to say anything, or if they'll be able to just come in and do it.' There were compliments from both of them for one boy who was 'working away there — smashing. You can hear his brain ticking. Straight into it'. There were also reproofs for those who 'should be sitting down and working by now, like this lad, look, he's away'. But it appeared that too many were still unable to 'just come in and do it'.

5.3   T: Well, I'd like to compliment some people who came in and worked very well. Some people came in straightaway, they remembered what they had to do. They saw the books and they saw the tray of booklets and they came in and got on with it and sorted themselves out : : : : If you come in and see the books out like that, and if Mr — doesn't give you any instructions, what should you do? : : : : What's the routine when you come in, what should you do?
       P: Sir, you get your books and start work. ((Starting work is then elaborated again by one of the teachers.))

At the other end of the lesson, packing up was also described with a detail that would soon be redundant. With the rooms in constant use, curriculum materials had to be returned to base quickly and quietly and with a minimum of supervision:

5.4   T: When we say pack up, you do this. Fold your book up, put your pens and pencils away. : : : : Because every lesson, we aren't going to say to you, 'Begin — now end.' We're just going to say, 'Right, pack up', and you put your booklet in there, put your book in there, put your pens and pencils away, and you're ready to go.

The aim of all this organizational activity was that the children should be able to 'go on as if I've said nothing to you at all : : : : Because the idea is that you should be able to come in and not have to ask anybody anything. That's what we're aiming for.' By the end of their third Humanities lesson, pupils should have been in no doubt about where the curriculum materials were, how they were to be collected, and how they were to be returned to base. The high proportion of teacher-talk devoted to these ends made the lessons seem very tightly controlled, but the intention was to establish conditions in which children accustomed (or so their new teachers thought) to doing things together would learn quickly to work independently. The critical importance of working, indicated by the frequency with which the word was used, was not yet accompanied by much explication of what kind of work it was to be. The pupils were sufficiently experienced in the ways of classrooms to know how to present themselves as busy — to appear to be reading, writing, or preparing to write. There might be some check later on the quantity and quality of the output, but for the moment the appearance of such activity was usually enough. Nor did the teachers seem to see any need to define in detail what working involved. It was more necessary for the moment to indicate that the *work-rate* was not always what it should be, as in the following example (the same teacher but on different occasions):

5.5   T: We're behind, so we've got to get a move on, this group. Not doing too
           well here.
      T: Come on men, you aren't half slow today.
      T: Now I want you to get on this morning, because we're a little behind
           the other group : : : : Right, put your hand up if you're not working.

As the term went on, varieties of work were spelled out more clearly, and these involved some kinds of learning with which pupils were *not* assumed to be already familiar. But what was emphasized initially was the searching out of answers readily available in the packaged materials.

(b) Getting at the facts

In the previous chapter, we indicated that the first-year work in Humanities was seen by those teaching it as an extended preparation for the more demanding activities generated from the 'Study of Man'. They regarded much of the early content especially as something of a holding operation which gave the children time to settle down. Working meant getting on quickly and quietly, preferably without the teacher's help. Therefore the tasks set had to be fairly closed so as to leave little scope for confusion. Pupils could find the answers by simply reading the appropriate section of the booklet, and they were told clearly how to set those answers out:

5.6   T1:   Right, we're starting new work, we'll need a new title, then.
      P: 'In the beginning.'
      T1:   The title, as George has just told us, will be 'In the beginning' because
            that's the title of the work that we're doing, that's the big main title.
      T2:   It's up here, Mr —.
      T1:   If you all look to the white board, you'll see the title in Mr —'s
            writing. All *your* writing will be better than that, Mr—'s quite honest
            about this.
      T2:   Mine's terrible writing, I didn't get taught properly at school, you
            see.

T₁: You'll notice Mr — is good at underlining, though — two nice straight lines done with a ruler under the title so that the page has a good clean beginning. The date to the right of the title. The date today is the 13th. And then what do we do? We've put the title, we've put the date . . .

P: Put question one.

T₁: No, we don't put question one straightaway.

P: Read up to question one in the booklet.

T₁: Yeah, the first thing that we do is to read through the booklet, is to read the information and look at the diagrams carefully. We did go through this with you last week so you should find this a quick and easy job. When you've read through the information, you'll come to worksheet A, and then you put question one and answer that. All on your own. We're going to try and work on our own this morning. If you need help, you put your hand up and Mr— or myself will come and help you.

This apparently rigid definition of what constituted finding out was not representative of teaching strategies later in the term, but it made it possible to hold the ring while various group and individual problems had time to emerge and be dealt with. The resulting predominance of administrative talk by the teachers was explicitly justified by the need to create conditions in which pupils could work on their own 'and not have to ask anybody anything'. But classroom tasks are never open to complete mechanization, and the normality of being stuck was also explicitly announced. Anybody who could not manage on his own had only to put up his hand and ask for help. This notion of the teacher as helper, as the first resource for those in difficulties, is so much taken for granted in classroom life that there was no need to elaborate on the nature of the help being offered.

This was so even when the pedagogical significance of the tasks had not yet been made clear. Getting at the facts was clearly important, but what were *Humanities* facts? What was learning to be like in that part of the curriculum? It would not have been sensible to have presented these beginners with an exposition of long-term aims. For much of what they were to do in that part of the school year, they would have to wait and see. The signalling of the appropriate learner roles was also largely implicit. How this signalling was *done* without actually being *said* is a question we take up later. But some things were put into words. We have seen how the answers to worksheet questions were presented as being already there, to be uncovered by reading the relevant material. Sometimes this simply meant filling in the right word. Interaction with pupils in difficulties was then channelled, quite overtly, towards getting them to use the label contained in the booklet. For example:

5.7   P: What do you do there?
       T: There? You read through it again if you've forgotten, and find out what happened when the earth was made. Now part of the earth — we think the earth was formed when part of it came away from the sun. So can you think of a word to get across the idea of it coming away from the sun? Now give me a word which means to come away from, can you? It's a simple word actually that we're after.

The quite lengthy game of 'hunt the label' which followed was later replayed with two other pupils. Though the routes differed in line and length, the destination was the same:

       T: The earth broke— that's all, it probably broke away from the sun as a whirling mass of gas. OK? Dead simple word, isn't it — you know, 'broke'. That's all we were after there.

These were the sharpest examples of the teacher's control over meanings being made explicit. More interesting were those occasions when the relative openness of what was said — for example, about a co-operative working out of ideas in which the teacher too would learn something — seemed to be contradicted by what was being *done*. We examine such sequences later in this chapter, and in Chapter 7. Clearly, invitations from the teacher to discuss working procedures or to discover new meanings can be dismissed as a matter of style rather than of substance, and there was a nice example of this in the second lesson we observed. Suggestions were invited as to how the giving out of books could be done more efficiently. Some of these were accepted as things 'we *could* do', but the teacher's own plan was spelled out in such detail that the suggestion which preceded it could only have been a convenient feed-line. The exposition ended, however, with the comment, 'We'll follow that young man's suggestion'. Such verbal gestures leave the teacher's control entirely intact (as in Henry Ford's celebrated offer, 'Any colour so long as it's black'). But even at this early stage in the pupils' career in Humanities, the ideological justification of 'working on your own' was sometimes spelled out:

5.8   P: Sir, I still can't find it. ((An item of information which he had been told to look up in an encyclopedia.))
       T: That one's no good. You're going to have to try the others. I'm not going to tell you which one. We want you to find out for yourself, 'cos you can do it. It's there. It might take you all lesson, but don't worry.

5.9   P: Sir, do we have to do that, or leave it out?
       T: No, this one. We want you to have a go at doing it yourself, rather than us doing it for you. Have a go at drawing that— turn your book side on. Try to draw it : : : :
       P: Sir, sir, what's the Milky Way?

T: I'm not going to tell you, because in there there are encyclopedias and one or two books about Space, so go in there, find the books which are about Space, and then use them to look it up. Do you know how to use an index in a book?

P: Yeah.

T: OK, if it takes you all lesson, it doesn't matter, 'cos you're finding it out for yourself.

This deflection of attention away from the teacher as the main source of facts is put into words because it is seen as involving for many children a significant departure from forms of learning to which they were accustomed. It also meant a considerable departure from traditional patterns of classroom communication.

(c) Talk, chatter, and silence

The existence of a central communication system means that whatever is being said requires the attention of all. Because of the prevalence of worksheets in the classrooms we observed, such centralization of talk was unusual. Those occasions when it *was* required were fairly explicitly identified, as was the level of private talk that could legitimately accompany work. We commented earlier that learning to behave in classrooms is very much a matter of knowing when and how to talk, and most of the deviance imputations in these lessons were concerned with (for example) paying attention, not interrupting, 'talking and not working', 'getting the chattering down so that people can work', and maintaining an appropriately quiet 'good working atmosphere'. Of the thirty-seven recorded occasions when pupils were reproved, individually or collectively, twenty-five directly identified transgressions of this kind. Many guide-lines were provided in how to communicate competently in the different stages of a lesson, each with its different rules.(5)

The most sharply marked stages, with the least ambiguous rules, were when a teacher was publicly announcing some organizational details or explaining an instructional item. Such occasions were unusually frequent in these early lessons so that they could quickly become *in*frequent. The following examples are taken from different lessons:

5.10 (a) T: Look, I can't talk if people are still working because that means you're not listening : : : Just a minute, I haven't told you to do it yet. Just sit still and listen. Somebody over there still isn't sitting still, they're fiddling around with a book. Somebody over there is fiddling with his bag.

(b) T1: Right, could you *all* listen please. *Everybody*. Oi, gentlemen! We'll just tell you quickly what we want you to do for homework, but I'd like everybody to listen, please. Even if you're behind me, listen : : : :

T2: Can I just check, Mr—? I've an idea there's one or two over here who didn't hear what you said, or didn't want to. ((Speaking to a pupil.)) It might be you we ask next. What have you got to do? What did Mr — tell you you've got to do?

P: ((Untranscribable.))

T2: He said something before that. You weren't listening. *You* weren't listening either, you were talking. You must listen to what's being said.

(c) T: OK, we'll start in a minute. We'll wait till everybody's quiet. What I want to do is to run through it with everybody to make sure that people understand what the two stories . . . *do you mind*, what was I just saying, John?

P: ((Mutters inaudibly.))

T: Right, you were busy talking, weren't you? Why? ((Silence.)) We've not got time to waste, John, we need to do this so that *everybody* knows what they're doing. So don't waste any more time, please.

At times like these, *everybody* must listen, and even a single defaulter has to be brought to order. At other times, 'everybody' may mean 'most of you', and 'silence' may mean 'not too much noise'. Pupils have to work out, from what they know of that teacher in that kind of situation, how large a silent majority will be acceptable to him, and how many (and how noisy) side-sequences will be tolerated. But there are occasions when 'everybody listening' means exactly that, and the literal application of the rule takes precedence even over working. Anything less wastes time.

The only other stage when real silence was consistently demanded was at the end of lessons. We noted earlier the relative rigidity with which full attention is demanded by teachers at the start and the finish of the lesson proper, as though to emphasize the sanctity of its boundaries. At Abraham Moss, the physical setting in the open area, the likelihood that children would arrive at different times, and the emphasis on 'working on your own' without being told to do so — all these conditions acted against any formalized beginning to the lesson. Indeed, having to call the whole group to order indicated a temporary breakdown in the routines of getting down to work. 'Packing up' was another matter. This had to be done quickly, and quietly, and together, and greater care was given to establishing and rehearsing the proper procedures.

During the lesson, while children were working on their own, some noise was permissible. Its legitimacy was made explicit in ways which provide a useful example of how meanings are embedded in a particular context. The following utterances represent all the definitions of a 'working noise' which the teachers provided in these lessons:

5.11   (a)   People are talking and not working.

(b)   I can hear people chattering instead of working. If you have to talk, whisper quietly.

(c)   There are still people chattering.

(d)   You're making too much noise at this table. You should be working.

(e)   Now the lads behind me, when they got their things they were still talking about five minutes afterwards. I think actually they were trying to sort out a problem. But if you've got to do that, talk with somebody about the work, do it quietly. I heard this racket going on behind me, and I thought they hadn't started working and they were disturbing the other people. So if you've got a question like that for your neighbour, keep it nice and quiet.

(f)   Put your hand up if you're stuck. Just one, just one person needs to see me. Could the others make sure they're working, please. Shhh. Still a bit of chattering. Let's get all the chattering down 'cos people can't work.

(g)   Er, there's a lot of chatter. Now come on, you've been asked very reasonably. If you can't get on, put your hand up. Stop all the chatter and all the talk about football and all the rest of it. We're having a Humanities lesson now — let's get on with it. ((A proper noise level is duly established.)) Now let's keep it like that, that's a good working atmosphere, that's great.

A number of interrelated definitions can be identified here. Talking quietly is not only compatible with work, it may be necessary to it; it is therefore part of a 'working atmosphere'. Quiet talk is likely to be heard by the teacher as talk relevant to the task in hand. A 'racket' not only disturbs the work of others, it is also likely to be irrelevant. Most economically, and both teachers were consistent in their usage, 'chattering' meant talking instead of working. It was talk *and not* work, clearly distinguished from talk *and* work.

Underlying these detailed rules about the proper forms of communication lay the teachers' right to decide on the appropriate talkers, listeners, and levels of noise. Pupils had to learn to listen on demand, and to monitor a working noise. They also had to talk on demand, to answer a question or contribute to a discussion. Discovering the necessary competence in that situation occurred within a framework provided by authoritative definitions of what *was* appropriate. The teacher's right to make most of the decisions may seem to be renounced by progressive teachers, and it may be lost in a sharp battle or a long war of attrition. But in the early encounters of a teacher with new pupils, it can normally be assumed to be there. In the rest of this chapter, we consider features of the interaction which were there without being put into words. But we should first emphasize that the details we have described appeared as persistent residues in later interaction. In an earlier example, we quoted a teacher complimenting those pupils 'who came in straightaway and *remembered* what they had to do . . . they came in and they got on with it and they sorted themselves out'. In the first lessons we recorded, the teachers had to treat such remembering as a problem. For example, a detailed recapitulation of how to work with the booklets ended with the following exchange:

5.12   T: Jane, why shouldn't you try and do the questions before you read the booklet?
         P: 'Cos you won't know the answers.
         T: Do you know that I bet you that in two weeks' time, we'll come back in here when we're doing another booklet and I bet you I have to say to somebody, 'You didn't read the booklet, did you?' Now can you all remember that?
         Pn: Yes, sir.
         T: I bet tuppence that there's somebody in this room in two weeks who has tried to do the questions without looking at the booklet.
         P: Tenpence, sir.
         T: No, I'm not rich. Tuppence.

When we returned to the school later in the year, the sorts of things that were being made explicit at the beginning were now being assumed by the teachers. Procedural details of how to begin work, and how to display to the teacher that work was indeed going on, were now known. For example, at the start of one lesson where the children were still chattering after several minutes, the teacher could say, 'Anne, get sorted now, please'. An outsider might have found this a highly ambiguous command, but it is unlikely that Anne did so. She would have been able to draw on previously explicated knowledge about how to begin Humanities lessons with this teacher in order to fill in the command in the appropriate way. Matters which had dominated the early recordings only got into words when common meanings were being challenged in some way (as in the example above), when something was going to be different this time, or when the teacher had some evidence that pupils did not understand. To take a very simple example, pupils normally began a new topic by drawing an illustrated title-page. But when they began work on Tristan da Cuhna, the teacher did not want this done and so had to make a different way of beginning explicit. They were to 'put the title "Tristan da Cunha" and just underline it and then start reading the book for today'. Everything else about beginning work could be left inexplicit, because they had had two terms' experience of what that activity meant. A similar explicitness became necessary when a pupil seemed not to understand a procedure which was no longer routinely spelled out. An example of this kind occurred when a child had difficulty with a multiple choice question in one of the booklets. It was assumed in the booklet, and by the teachers, that pupils knew how to deal with questions like this. But on this occasion, the teacher had to put into words information that was assumed in the very form of the question: 'Now what you have to do is to finish off each of the sentences by choosing one of the answers. So you begin the first one, "A community is . . .", then you finish off with either (a) or (b) or (c).'

In each of these three examples (the challenge, the different rule *this* time, and the reminder), the teacher was unable to go on to the substantive content of the curriculum until a common meaning for the appropriate working procedures had been established. Whereas our first transcripts were dominated by this procedural talk, it had largely faded out in the later recordings. But it was just as much there as before, as an unstated back cloth to the interaction. In the rest of the chapter, we argue that the construction of this background knowledge was itself dependent on more general knowledge which the children were assumed to possess already. In order to follow what their new teachers were talking about, they had to know already how to listen properly, how to follow instructions, how to do what they were told without argument. This knowledge of how to behave in classrooms was presupposed in the process of procedural settling in.

2 Procedural Competence and Relationship Knowledge

The construction of particular ways of working was supported by a framework of traditional teacher—pupil relationships which did not, at that stage, need to be spelled out. The details were what needed to be *said*. Other, more general, information about classroom life was not transmitted explicitly; it was assumed that pupils would make sense of what *was said* because they would fit it into their general understanding of what classrooms are like. What seemed to us to have happened in these first lessons (among much else!) was that the teachers were relying on this general knowledge to provide a basic interpretive framework within which various details could be elaborated. The underlying structure of classroom purposes and relationships was, for the time being, taken as read.

It is obvious that everything cannot be done at once — that situations are defined sequentially, not simultaneously. Indeed, the process is continuous, since no situation is comprehensively defined once and for all. What was interesting about the early lessons we observed was the extent to which it was the *details* which were filled in. Pupils were assumed to be competent in generalities but necessarily incompetent in particulars, and so the main weight of words fell (for example) on establishing how the booklets were to be distributed, how written work was to be set out, and how lessons were to begin and end. We are not arguing that the meaning of other activities was immediately apparent to the children, but that they assumed that what was going on *had* meaning even where its significance was temporarily unclear. About much that was happening, there seemed to be a willing suspension of incomprehension, a willingness to believe that it would all make sense eventually. It was therefore possible to settle them down to work with an ease that would otherwise have been surprising.

The preceding account was partly derived from an intensive study of the lesson transcripts. But always at the back of our minds were the ideas discussed at the end of Chapter 3, and we returned to Cicourel's work in particular with new appreciation of its insights. Our account can therefore be translated into more theoretical form. Cicourel comments that in an initial encounter between strangers, each may accept the other temporarily as an individual before and during the exchange of information about more general characteristics like occupation. This is not what happens in classrooms because the relevant categories of teacher and pupil are obvious. But these categories only provide general guide-lines, *not* whole sets of ready-made answers to any problems that may arise in the interaction. They *do* allow teacher and pupils, however, to trust their environment not to produce too many surprises, and to make sense of particular items of behaviour by fitting them into what they take to be normal forms of interaction in that kind of setting. They make sense of information from the immediate situation by articulating it with more general knowledge of that kind of situation, and they assume that others are doing so in broadly similar ways. Thus they seem to agree on how to interact even when they have not yet indicated 'any explicit grounds or basis for the agreement'.(6) This agreement must not be made to look too easy, nor its scope too wide. Conventional accounts of classroom roles usually seem arid and unreal because they try to cover too much of the interaction with detailed prescriptions of what must, may, and cannot be done. Such a blueprint would be applicable, if at all, only to the most ritualized of encounters. It is much more useful to ask how the participants in highly status-marked settings like classrooms sustain a sense of normal interaction through all the fine details of what occurs, how they generate appropriate responses to frequently and rapidly changing situations, and how they search the behaviour of others for evidence about what is really going on.

As we have argued already, the teachers we observed seemed to be assuming that they already shared with their pupils many definitions of 'proper' classroom behaviour. They put into words those things they expected to be new, or different, or that seemed to cause problems. We also commented that in these early lessons, open disobedience was rare. But there were many occasions when children seemed unclear about the precise form or content of classroom activities, and we have seen how the teachers cleared the way to deal with individual difficulties. As we have described them so far, these can be seen as procedural or surface problems. But any separation of surface from base is merely a descriptive convenience. As the teacher announces and elaborates detailed rules of procedure, he is *also* announcing and confirming his right to make such decisions. He does not have to make this basic right explicit before he can proceed to act on it. It is no less real for being contained within what he says, and in how his pupils respond. The nature of most of the *authority talk* in these early lessons documents our argument that the process of settling in depended on certain basic assumptions about teacher–pupil relationships, assumptions which revolve around the notion of the teacher as being in charge.(7) We saw earlier how much of the classroom talk was explicitly about procedural details so that a common understanding of how to work in that context could be established. Once these details had been made explicit, they largely fell out of the talk, providing an essential background if teachers and pupils were to interact in orderly and consistent ways. Much of what was actually said in later lessons could be regarded as an index to the wider meanings previously established, and only by filling them in in the same way could the participants know what was meant. But we have also argued that even in their first lessons in a new school, pupils were assumed to know *already* how to make basic sense of classroom interaction by fitting procedural details into more general patterns. When a boy asked a teacher, 'Sir, what's the Milky Way?', the very question subsumed a reciprocity of perspectives about how to proceed through a worksheet, how to identify the facts required by a particular task, and how to address a teacher properly. But the question also implied acceptance of the teacher as helper, as a source of authoritative information, and of the pupil's duty to follow the official curriculum. It is this basis of classroom interaction that we now consider solely in relation to the first lessons we recorded. Its appearances in a wider range of instructional encounters are then examined in the two chapters which follow, while the concluding chapter extends the general analysis by relating our own research to some other studies of how social relationships determine the ways in which language is used.

3   Teacher Authority and Classroom Talk

In orderly classrooms, teachers rarely make their *power* obvious. But almost all their talk, and their pupils' talk, assumes their *authority*. This distinction between power and authority distinguishes between an enforced conformity and something which is normally granted by those being told what to do.(8) Power-talk involves open threats and frequent imperatives. Authority-talk covers all those instances when the teacher avoids making his control obvious by (for example) couching a command in the form of a request, and when pupils *routinely* confirm the teacher's control by accepting or appearing to work towards his frame of reference. The power aspect of the relationship may then be apparent only in the speed with which teachers act when they perceive that pupils are not addressing them (openly *or* implicitly) as being in charge. Thus pupils who 'can't be bothered to listen to me while I'm talking' will be 'invited' to leave because they have committed a very basic classroom offence. There was a highly explicit statement of the teacher's control in the second full lesson we observed:

5.13   T: Ah — I should only have to ask you once to be quiet and then everybody should be hushed straightaway. Think of what time it is now, and what goes on next. What happens if you aren't quiet the first time we ask? ((Pause.)) Well, it's break now, isn't it, so if we have to ask you to be quiet all the time you start losing break. What's your name?

   P: David.

   T: I'd like to compliment David because he's the only person in this room who did *exactly* what he was asked to do at the beginning.

As we have seen, this statement occurred at a stage in the lesson when full attention was especially likely to be demanded. Such explicit and extended instances of calling the children to order were rarely needed. The teachers' authority was routinely recognized by the ways in which the children listened and worked and sought help at the proper times and in the proper ways, and avoided too much chatter. It was most pervasively recognized in the normally very unequal distribution of public talk, and in acceptance of a formal allocation by the teacher of turns at speaking. In these first lessons, the right of the teachers to do most of the talking themselves was not something that had to be announced or justified. Along with the right to nominate pupils to speak, it was tacitly conceded. Almost all pupil contributions were therefore responses to a teacher's question. The following represent all those contributions in four lessons which were not *directly* elicited in this way, and which can therefore be seen as some kind of communicational initiative:

5.14   Sir, there's someone in my place.
She hasn't got a pen or pencil.
Sir, do you have to put the names of the planets in order?
Sir, should we start like that?
Sir, can she be monitor to collect our work?
Sir, is this Humanities? ((This was geographical, not an epistemological question.))
Where's the booklets?
What's the date, sir?
Sir, did you read about the shark? ((As we will see, this initiative did lead to something like a genuine conversation.))
Sir, me friend's just found me other book.
Sir, how does the planet system work?
Do we write it all down?
What did you mean by 'Make sure you read the instructions'?
Sir, what did you mean by 'Neat quick work'?
Sir, do you go straight on to the next one?
Sir, do you write a complete list of planets?
Sir, do we read that?
Sir, have we got to do a poem?
Sir, I don't understand this.
Sir, I'm stuck with this one.
Sir, sir, sir, what do you do there?
Sir, what's the Milky Way?
Sir, can I read?
We've got little rooms like that.
Sir, her earing's come out.

We saw earlier how asking a question is often a way of seizing the initiative by defining what the next piece of interaction is to be about. But almost none of the initiatives listed above do this. Whether asking for instructions, clarification, permission, or decision, they stay firmly within the teacher's frame of reference. Even taken out of context, they constitute implicit recognition that the teacher was indeed in charge. The acceptance of a subordinate role is apparent in the willingness to seek out directions — to wait to be told.

The normal hierarchical relationship of teacher and pupil is usefully illustrated by comparing the following sequences involving the same teacher. The first is taken from a lesson about the opposing forces of Yin and Yang in Chinese mythology, Yang being 'powerful and warm like a man' while Yin was described in the booklet as 'dark, weak, cold, more like a woman'. The second encounter was something of a side-sequence before the lesson proper began.

5.15   T: What do you think of that, this idea that the woman was dark, cold? What do you think? Do you agree with it?

P: I do.

T: You do. ((Laughter.)) Hang on, let's have a girl. Sylvia, come on, you seem to be willing to talk.

P: ((Mutters.))

T: Come on, what do you think of that idea, Sylvia?

P: Rubbish.

T: Rubbish. ((Laughter.)) *Why* is it rubbish? Or any of the girls, why do you think it's rubbish?

5.16   P: Sir, did you read about that shark?

T: No, what happened?

P: He was eighteen foot.

T: Where?

P: They caught it. They got it with about five harpoons. You know, it was in a fishing book.

T: Just recently or . . .

P: Yeah.

T: Where did they do it?

P: Well, I don't know where, I just read it. And it was two foot short of Jaws — it was massive.

T: No, I didn't — I haven't read it, actually.

P: Me dad's mate gets all fishing books, and when he's finished with them he gives them to me 'cos I like fishing, and, um, it was on the back page. I'll bring it along and show you, sir.

T: Yeah, bring it along.

In the first extract, the teacher's turns really need no identifying label. He clearly owns the interaction. It is his idea to which the children must respond, and somebody has to be willing to speak to it. The first volunteer has his offer acknowledged but not taken up, and a second volunteer has to take part. Her initial unwillingness to do so has to be covered by at least a token (if inaudible) response. Now such an exchange *might* occur in a conversation in mixed company with one over-zealous disputant, but common-sense tells us that it would be most unlikely because it is too obviously and unilaterally controlled. In classrooms, however, it is a typical exchange. The second example is much closer to conversation, which was earlier defined as occasions where communicative rights are more or less equally shared, and where there are few predetermined limits on how topics and turns are to be decided. There was nothing in the previous interaction to authorize the topic of sharks. The boy's initial question is completely outside the official framework of the lesson, and it does not presume that the teacher already knows the answer. The teacher then asks four genuine questions himself, while a further contribution ('I haven't read it, actually') still leaves the floor open to the pupil. Though the teacher has the last word in the exchange, it is the pupil who terminates the topic. Indeed, the pupil retains topical control throughout, partly by side-stepping some questions so that he can supply those facts he *does* know. In normal classroom interaction, such side-stepping would either be disallowed or else the teacher would choose to hear a relevant response by imposing his own meanings on what had been said.

Normal interaction, reflecting and reinforcing the teacher's authority, will be illustrated finally by one of the several instances of class teaching in the early lessons. The pupils know at the outset that this part of their work is called 'Life begins in the Sea'. After distributing a box of fossils around the class, the teacher begins by saying:

> Could anybody tell me what — *shh* — tell me and tell the rest of us what you can see in the particular piece of stone that you've got? Put your hands up please and tell me. Yes?

His question elicits ten separate statements (e.g. 'It's all little, well, dead animals'), the whole sequence of which is quoted in Chapter 7. Up to this point, all that has been required is description. Although one utterance is received as a 'good description', all the others are accepted by being repeated by the teacher. This persistent repetition, usually of the form as well as the content, is strikingly unlike conversation, and it makes clear who is managing the interaction even when evaluation is witheld.

5.17 T: Right, OK. Now hanging on to those pieces of stone, um, all I'm going to tell you is, and some of you already know — well, can anybody tell me what's on those stones? What's on them? What are they?

P: Fossils.

T: Right, OK. Can you tell us what fossils are, do you think?

P: Sir, sir, a long time ago — and there was animals and when they died, er, the rain and wind came over them and then the bodies disappeared and left the shells and that.

T: Good. Why do you think the bodies disappeared and the shells stayed?

Pn: Sir, sir, they rotted.

T: And what about the shells?

P: Sir, they got harder — er, when the clay dried, they made marks in the clay.

T: Right.

P: The clay dried hard.

T: Right, OK, thank you. Can anybody add anything to that at all? It's a very good description. Can anybody add anything? Yes?

P: Sir, living creatures set in rock.

T: Good. Now he's right in what he said in actual fact, that when these creatures were floating around in the sea — when they died, they sank to the bottom. Now this particular creature I've got in my hand here was called an ammonite.

P: Sir, there's one in the book.

T: There's a picture of one in the book on page 3. Would you like to turn to that picture on page 3 — can you see it, that whirly-twirly thing? Have you got it?

P: That one?

T: That's it. Now, what happened when this fish died — let me draw a little picture of it here, I always like drawing these things 'cos they're easy to draw : : : :   now what happened was that inside there used to live a little snail. What's the animal, what's that thing called on *Magic Roundabout* that lives in a . . .

Pn: Sir, sir, Brian.

T: That's it, Brian. Well, this ammonite was like a great-great-great-great-great grandfather of Brian because inside it used to live a little bit like a small snail and this shell was the home where it used to live. Why do you think the creature used to live inside a shell like that?

Pn: ((Numerous bids to speak.))

T: No, put your hands up please. Er, Carl?

P: For protection.

T: What does protection mean? Any idea, Carl?

P: Sir, to stop other things hurting it.

T: Right, stops other things hurting it. Now if it came out of its shell and waggled along the sea bed, what would happen to it? Yes?

P: It might get ate.

T: It might get eaten by something else, yeah. Um, why do you think this is made out of stone now? It's quite heavy, isn't it — weighs about a pound. It's a . . . er, I won't tell you how a fossil happened yet, you'll be learning about that later, but why isn't — er, why don't we find the remains of the creature inside here?

P: It would have rotted away.

T: It would have rotted away. Why didn't the shell rot away?

P: Sir, because it's too hard.

T: It's too hard, good. Um, if I die tomorrow and I float to the bottom of the sea — don't cheer ((pupils duly cheer)) — if I float to the bottom of the sea, what parts — if you were a scientist and you came along in a couple of million years and you looked for my fossil — what parts of my body would you find? Hasan?

P: Sir, the skeleton.

T: The bones, in other words. What other bits would you find?

P: Sir, your watch.

T: Oh, the watch would rot away. What other bits would you find?

P: Er, probably an old shoe or something.

T: No, no, you'd find my bones but what else would you find?

P: (Some tiny . . .)

T: No — *millions* of years, this is.

P: Teeth.

T: *Right*, yes, your bones, your teeth, and maybe your nails. So you find your bones and your teeth — um, *that*'s what you find of your fossils. Now the bones you're looking at . . .

This interaction follows the normal class-teaching form. The teacher takes every other turn, and usually allocates the intervening turns. He does most of the talking. He asks questions to which he clearly knows the answers, because he elaborates or evaluates each reply, and these replies are absorbed into his developing exposition. Most pupil contributions are so short that they seem to be made for instant elaboration by the teacher. The controlled allocation of turns is inseparable from the shaping of meanings towards a predetermined objective. The whole sequence can be seen as organized around progressively more complex answers to the question, 'What are fossils?', a question prepared for by the previous exchanges about what they looked like. The pupils' *responding* contributions seem to reflect their perception that the teacher is doing the telling, and in relation to the further question of how fossils happened he explicitly announces that the telling will come latei.

This brief account of the sequence was deliberately framed in ways which we considered in detail in Chapter 2. But it can also be seen as a typical working out of the teacher's authority. The teacher provides the framework into which pupil-talk is fitted, and that talk is assessed according to the closeness of fit. Brief pupil contributions are taken as being representative of the group, and the interaction then proceeds *as though* the other pupils either knew already, or shared the same and *now corrected* inadequacies as those who spoke.(9) In its orderliness, and in the shaping of meanings, the interaction can be seen as the managed product of one of the participants.

Class teaching of this kind was a rare occurrence. As we have seen, the predominant teaching technology was that of pupil-directed work, with the teachers performing mainly as trouble-shooters and problem-solvers. In the chapter which follows, we examine the kinds of interaction which resulted. Did the management of meanings then take very different forms, and was it markedly less of a one-way process? The lesson from which we quoted at length was only a prelude to more individualized forms of learning. Shortly before the end of it, the teacher said, 'Will you just follow this with me? We'll just get this stuck in our minds, and then I'll leave you all to it.' In what ways *were* pupils 'left to it' in the lessons which we observed?

Chapter 5: Notes and References

1   Recordings later in the school year showed this girl as an active talker.

2   Bernstein (1973), *Class, Codes and Control*, vol. 1, p. 201.

3   Smith and Geoffrey (1968), *The Complexities of an Urban Classroom*, chap. 3. One of their main reflections on classroom analysis (pp. 228–50) was that correlating overt teacher-behaviour and pupil-reaction was often unsound because what the child was responding to was often buried deep in past interaction, and maintained 'mostly through reputation and rare overt comment or act by the teacher'.

4   The notion of 'busyness' is discussed in detail in Sharp and Green (1975), *Education and Social Control*, pp. 121–5.

5   Hargreaves *et al*. (1975), *Deviance in Classrooms*, pp. 89–105, make a detailed analysis of the 'changing contexts of lessons' and of the 'switch-signals' used by teachers to switch on and off the relevant rules. They suggest that the clarity of such signals is an important feature of good discipline. A similar point is made by Walker and Adelman (1975b), *A Guide to Classroom Observation*, p. 17.

6   Cicourel (1973), *Cognitive Sociology*, p. 40. The first two chapters of this book had a strong influence on our analysis. There is also some common ground with Stebbins's notion of 'standard meanings', habitual definitions which participants are aware they share with others, which provide entrants to a situation with enough of a working consensus to be going on with. See Stebbins (1975), *Teachers and Meaning*, pp. 16–17.

7   As we argue more fully in Chapter 8, these are not assumptions which the pupils could necessarily have explicated in interviews. We are suggesting that they must have been there for the interaction to have taken the course it did, and that the talk can only be read properly by taking them into account. What we have called 'relationship knowledge' is comparable with the use by Hargreaves *et al*. (1975), pp. 94–104, of 'relational rules' to refer not to rules actually invoked in classroom interaction, but to their own 'highly condensed abstractions' from those which *were* so invoked. Their relational rules include 'doing what(ever) you're told', and 'co-operating' by (for example) answering teachers' questions and contributing to discussion.

8   For an extended statement of this distinction between power and authority, see Gerth and Mills (1970), *From Max Weber*, chapter 9. We return to these concepts in Chapter 8.

9   That teachers often assume the very knowledge they are intending to teach is argued by Cicourel, pp. 315–18, and Mehan, p. 114, in Cicourel *et al*. (1974), *Language Use and School Performance*.

Chapter 6

Teaching and Learning as the Creation of Meanings

1 Classroom Knowledge and the Reciprocity of Perspectives

When we engage in some form of social interaction, like a conversation, we assume that the situation we face means the same to us as to the person (or persons) we are talking to. We assume that we both draw on the same body of commonsense knowledge to interpret what the other says and does. Yet, because we are all individuals with different biographies and possibly separate interests, we may well have different perspectives on the situation at hand. But if we are to maintain social interaction, we will either have to gloss over or suspend these differences, or else establish new meanings we both can accept.(1) What the Humanities teachers were doing in the first weeks of the autumn term was explicitly establishing a common sense of classroom organization. In Chapter 5 we demonstrated how this organizational talk was itself dependent on another body of knowledge — about classroom relationships — which teachers assumed they already held in common with their pupils. Their organizational talk subsumed within it, and was dependent for its comprehensibility on, this common relationship knowledge. After the first few weeks a reciprocity of perspectives about classroom organization was assumed too, and as long as that assumption was maintained, explicit references to procedure largely disappeared from the transcripts. That too could become part of the background knowledge participants were assumed to fill in appropriately when they engaged in curriculum talk.

Despite the fact that teachers and pupils assume a reciprocity of perspectives when talking about organizational and disciplinary work, they both assume that filling in the right meanings is a problem when it comes to the material to be learned. In this chapter we will show that teachers assume that pupils will not know what material means until they have been taught — until, for example, they have had a lead lesson, or been told what to look out for in the booklets. Pupils are likely to assume this too, and until they have been taught they suspend anything they already know about the subject matter. They must accept that they are 'ignorant' until they have taken over the teacher's system of meanings.(2)

In any piece of social interaction, it may become apparent that the participants do not have a reciprocity of perspectives. In the course of conversation, they may become aware that each means something different by a key term. If the difference is too obtrusive, it becomes a stumbling-block to the conversation; they must give their attention to it, and either establish a working definition or else change the subject. In talk between equals, neither has the right to insist on *his* definition or the obligation to wait for a ruling. But in most classrooms, academic meanings are the province of the teacher. The pupil will normally suspend any knowledge he has about the subject until he has found out the teacher's frame of reference, and moved (or appeared to move) into it. For the academic curriculum to proceed, a reciprocity of meanings has to be established. But in the unequal relationship between most teachers and pupils, the movement is nearly always in one direction; the pupil has to step into the teacher's system of meanings and leave them relatively undisturbed.(3) Being taught usually means suspending your own interpretations of the subject matter and searching out what the teacher means. Thus the very process of learning demonstrates and maintains the authority relationship, because the pupil is nearly always attempting to move into the teacher's world of meanings. The pupil's suspension of his own interpretation may be so complete that if he cannot understand what the material means to the teacher, then it becomes literally meaningless for himself.

The following extract illustrates this point. A boy was stuck on the question, 'Why do you think the Abraham Moss Centre is called a community centre?', and called the teacher over to help him.

6.1   T: Well, Abraham Moss is a community centre, isn't it? Now why do people come here?
      P: To work.
      T: What else? Not only — I mean, you come to work, yeah, but there are other things as well.
      P: Help.
      T: To get help, yes. OK. What else?
      P: ((Silence.))
      T: Name some other parts of the Centre.
      P: ((Mumbles.))
      T: Pardon?
      P: The gym.

Here the pupil is having difficulty answering questions about the very place in which he has spent a large part of his life for some months past. He must have extensive knowledge about the Centre. But in this context, he sets this knowledge aside and tries to search out the particular meanings which the teacher is after. The suspension of his own knowledge is so complete that he gives only monosyllabic replies — which he hopes, perhaps, can be slotted into whatever the teacher has in mind — and eventually falls into silence. As so often when there is something to be learned, teacher and pupil do not assume a reciprocity of perspectives. They do not assume that the material or the question means the same to them, and that the pupil will therefore be able to fill in the 'right' background meanings. The same meaning has to be *achieved*, and in most teaching this involves moving towards whatever the teacher will accept and validate.

It is possible, however, to look at this pupil's difficulty in a different way. Rather than setting aside his existing knowledge, he is perhaps being faced with a new situation. His silence might be because he has never before had to think about *why* people come to the Centre; this has not been a problem for him. This would frequently be the case with more technical subjects, when pupils are confronting new knowledge on matters which are initially meaningless to them. But even when they are on more familiar ground, a persistent boundary between classroom knowledge and everyday knowledge may lead them to search out meanings in line with what the teacher wants rather than to look to themselves and their own past experience, which might throw some light on the topic.(4) As we will argue in more detail later, the novelty of the task confronting them may not be that the content is new, but that it has to be formulated in unusual ways or with unusual explicitness. As in the example already cited, they may also be required to consider as a problem something that they had previously taken for granted. In either case, they will have to work, in order to generate the same framework of meanings as the teacher has.

The ways in which pupils move into the teacher's system of meanings can be illustrated by looking in detail at the following example. A boy had got stuck on the question, 'Work out using the scale how wide the island is to the nearest mile', and had called the teacher over to him for help. The question involved looking at a map reproduced in the booklet, referring to a scale marked out in miles and kilometres, and then measuring the island.

6.2 T: You know what a scale is?
     P: Sir, yeah.

T: Right. ((Points to the scale.)) What's that letter there?
P: One.
T: That letter?
P: Two.
T: Have you measured the distance between them?
P: Sir, yeah.
T: And how far is it?
P: Sir, one centimetre.
T: No. What's the distance between one and two on the scale?
P: Sir, in miles?
T: Yeah.
P: Sir, a mile.
T: No. What's the distance on the ruler?
P: Twenty millimetres.
T: What's that — convert twenty millimetres into centimetres.
P: Ten centimetres.
T: *Two* centimetres. Look, turn that ((*the ruler*)) round. It's *two* centimetres, right. So one mile equals how far?
P: Er, two centimetres.
T: Can you work out the distance?
P: Yes, sir.
T: What's the scale again?
P: Er, two centimetres to every mile.
T: Right, one mile equals . . .?
P: Two centimetres.
T: And then you can work it out?
P: Yeah.
T: Get it right. Do it slow and get it right. ((Teacher moves off.))

Here we can suggest that while the pupil may have come across the notion of a scale before, he recognizes that he does not know how to work out this particular question. He does not know what it is supposed to mean. At the end of the sequence we assume, as does the teacher, that the pupil has a new perspective on what the question wants. By following the teacher through a series of operations, he has come to see it in a new light; he now understands what is involved, because he apparently sees it in the way the teacher does. In this process of moving to the teacher's meaning, he offers possible answers of his own but is willing to abandon these if they are not confirmed. His first answer to the question about the distance between the two points — 'Sir, one centimetre' — would have been settled on as *the* answer if it had been confirmed. But it is wrong, and he has to try again. To narrow the area of search, the teacher asks a different question which implicitly provides a clue.

T: No. What's the distance between one and two on the scale?
P: Sir, in miles?

The pupil seems to recognize that he is not 'with' the teacher, and so makes suggestions which force the teacher to do more of the work. Further tentative answers are offered, which again are not confirmed.(5) In the end, the teacher has to *tell* him, but he does not tell him the answer. Rather, he leads him to the edge of it. Through the interaction, by suggesting possible meanings and then abandoning these as they are seen to be wrong, the pupil has come to see the question more in the way it was intended in the booklet — he has entered into the teacher's framework of meanings.

What we want to suggest is that this process of moving pupils towards the teacher's meanings, and maintaining them there, is at the heart of most teaching. Even in the more open environment being developed at Abraham Moss, pupils still have to suspend their own meanings and generate new ones in line with those implied by the teacher. This is not to say that some teaching technologies are not more efficient, and more flexible, than others. But essentially the same process is taking place. It involves pupils in producing tentative suggestions which may then be abandoned or locked in in the light of further clues from the teacher.

To present this view so bluntly is to risk diminishing the quality of much of the teaching we observed, and we return in the next chapter to its superiority to traditional teaching even within the framework of knowledge transmission, and to the considerable diversity of methods employed. It also risks making that process look altogether too easy. We therefore turn at this point to consider some of the major problems involved.

2 From Difficulties to Problems

As experts teachers have specialist meanings for the material that they teach, and learning involves the pupils' generating the same specialist interpretive frames. By interacting with teachers and with the written content of the curriculum pupils have to learn to interpret different aspects of their environment as physics, maths, music, or in this case Humanities.(6) But if pupils are to learn, if they are to take over and use these specialist meanings, they cannot be simply transmitted. Pupils have to build up or generate the same meanings from the evidence provided in the textbook or from what the teacher says. As we saw in the last example, if the pupil finds his proposed interpretation wrong, if it does not fit the facts as defined by the teacher, he abandons it and attempts to generate a new framework.

This process of generating specialist meanings from evidence pro-vided by the teacher is at the heart of most academic learning, but for most of the time it is hidden from view. Ethnomethodology has shown that whenever any of us want to understand something new we usually begin with an assumption that some sort of understanding is possible. We then propose tentative theories which we will abandon or change as necessary while at the same time we continue to reinterpret the facts. Some we will come to see in a new light and we will emphasize certain aspects of them, while others we will perhaps consider less important and we will push them to the back of our minds. Eventually, by this documentary process we achieve some sort of fit between our theory and the facts as we perceive them.(7)

Unfortunately, this generative process usually goes on inside our heads — we do not always talk it out. The same is true in the classroom. Pupils have to work to generate some sort of understanding of what the teacher means (though the process is simpler than in everyday life because the teacher unilaterally defines what the facts are), yet here too most of the interpretive process is hidden from view. It does not usually get into words. Barnes has demonstrated that in certain circumstances pupils can be encouraged to engage in exploratory talk amongst themselves and talk through these interpretive processes.(8) Unfortunately, because we only recorded the teachers we do not know if this sort of exploratory talk occurred in Abraham Moss classrooms. This interpretive work will also come to the surface when pupils have a problem. Pupils and teachers will then have to put into words what usually goes on behind the scenes. Concentrating on how teachers and pupils recognize and deal with problems has therefore become a major source of interest for us for it clearly demonstrates the process by which pupils generate meanings; we can see how a reciprocity of academic meanings is achieved. In other words we can see how people learn.

How much of what teachers say is being understood, or is already understood, by their pupils? How much pupil knowledge is already within the appropriate frame of reference, and how much new knowledge is being taken? In normal class teaching, finding the answers to these questions is a haphazard business. A few pupils answer questions; and this can give the impression that everyone understands. It is not until the teacher looks at the pupils' written work that he discovers how much of his cherished exposition went over the heads of many of his class. To overcome this difficulty, teachers employ a number of evidential procedures to find out if the class is following them. They may ask questions, or simply monitor pupils' looks and glances to see how much attention they are paying. But this is often doubtful evidence. As John Holt suggests, pupils are highly skilled at hiding the fact that they do not understand.

In resource-based learning, the evidential procedures can be more intensive. Largely released from the role of teller, the teacher has far more time for problem-solving. Indeed, this becomes his major function. He deals with a barrage of questions — some procedural, some to do with equipment and resources, and others to do with the substantive content of the lesson. Most of these contacts are initiated by pupils, though in his quieter moments the teacher himself initiates contacts with pupils whom he has not seen for a while or who do not seem to be working well. The demands on his time make it necessary to assume that if there is no pressing evidence of problems, then the children are working satisfactorily and understanding what they are doing. This assumption was put into words in an early lesson with first-year pupils. The group were asked if they had any problems in 'getting on'. Only four children put up their hands. After a pause, the teacher said, 'Now does that mean that everybody else except Peter, Paul, Abdul, and Shirley can carry on? ((Pause.)) Right.' He was asking them if *not* putting up their hands meant what he took it to mean, and he took their silence as evidence that they could indeed 'carry on'.

This notion of evidence is important in understanding how the teacher diagnoses the problems of pupils who do come up to him. His first task is to find out where the pupil is, what his precise difficulties are. He has to build up some conception of a problem, and this process of formulation, of making a problem from the pupil's less specific difficulty, is an integral part of providing a solution. We have argued that pupils frequently suspend any meanings which classroom topics may have had for them in the past, and search out the way the teacher sees it. The initial statement of the difficulties being encountered may be very non-specific. For example, this pupil was working on a question about the concept of community:

6.3   P: Sir, about the people.
       T: What about the people?
       P: They all work together?
       T: Of course, a group of people all living and working together in the same area — so a community is what, then?

The teacher quickly builds up some notion of what problem the pupil has. The pupil's first utterance is highly ambiguous, even to the teacher, and he is asked to expand it. When he does so, the teacher assumes that he now understands what the difficulty is, and he elaborates, 'They all work together?' into 'a group of people living and working in the same area'.(9) This elaboration of the pupil's statement has introduced two new features of a community: that it involves *living* as well as working together, and that it involves people doing these things in the *same area*.

So we can assume that the teacher has engaged in a documentary process by fitting the pupil's initial ambiguous utterance into some category of normal difficulties about what communities are. Since he gets no counter-evidence from the pupil that he is wrong in his assumption that this is where the problem lies, he goes on to integrate the pupil's expanded utterance into this new 'telling'. In a sense he has defined and solved his own problem.

In this section, the teacher seems to be acting as a kind of detective. He integrates his evidence of the pupil's difficulty into some form of normal problem, but, of course, as each case is unique he is creating or at least extending his notion of what a normal problem is at the same time. In this lesson the teacher had already established an idea that normal problems related to the concept of community. The course material was directed to developing an understanding of it, and one of the set questions was explicitly concerned with it. In the course of the lesson, a number of other pupils appeared to have similar difficulties. The teacher therefore quickly recognized their problems. In medical parlance, it was the most available diagnosis of trouble because there was a lot of it about.

The context (in this case the study of communities) therefore determined how the teacher heard the pupil's query and how he constructed a problem from it; it provided him with a theme around which to document the pupil's initial rather confused statement. In the early lessons with new pupils, queries were often heard as indicating that they did not understand how work was to be organized. An ambiguous question like 'Sir, what do we do there?' was likely to be heard not as a question about the content of the lesson but as a question about how to use the booklets. On this occasion, the teacher's reply was, 'There, you read through it again and find out what happened when the earth was made.' As pupils became more accustomed to working independently teachers were more likely to assume that they knew about working procedures, and the 'same' question would be heard as an indication of some semantic difficulty.

A more persistently normal problem related to difficulties with reading. For example:

6.4   T: How do you find the reading in that one, John?
      P: All right.
      T: What's the answer to the first question, then?
      P: Tristan lies to the south of the equator.
      T: Good.

On this occasion the teacher suspended his judgement about whether the boy could cope with the reading until he had heard some evidence.

He then took the fact that the boy could answer the question correctly as an indication that, at least for the moment, he could indeed cope. The teacher had established that one sort of normal problem — in general, and for this boy in particular — was difficulty with reading. This was a main criterion for distinguishing between pupils and the level of work that they could cope with.

In suggesting that teachers often seemed to type pupils in terms of their ability to read, we do not want to underestimate the complexity of their understanding.(10) One advantage of the resource-based method of instruction is that teachers have the time to interact with individual children, and there is more opportunity for each to see the other as a person.(11) Nevertheless, reading ability is obviously critical to the successful operation of this method of teaching. In the context of a wide range of more general abilities and a heavy emphasis on pupils working on their own, reading is *the* strategic skill. The teachers were constantly having to monitor how well pupils were coping with the booklets, and reading skills therefore became a central feature in getting to know them and in comparing one with another. As we have seen, they were also the basis for producing several levels of curriculum material. 'Difficulties with reading' was therefore one of the most readily available definitions of a normal problem in these classrooms, for it was one that all the teachers explicitly recognized and talked about and it was central to the success of their teaching.

We do not want to give the impression that these normal or typical problems were hard-and-fast categories into which pupils' difficulties could be slotted. In fact, the contrary is the case. In the first place, teachers had to create an understanding of what normal problems were likely to be and extend and refine their notions in order to incorporate each individual *instance* that they met.(12) Some of these patterns came to be seen as persistent and general, like difficulties with reading, and teachers became quite expert at identifying them.(13) The more often they came across a problem the more concrete the category became, but they would still have actively to interpret each case as an example of their normal problem and perhaps extend their idea of what, for example, a reading difficulty was so that it included this particular case.(14) Other problems, like the child below who often asked silly questions, were more difficult to understand and as the teacher explained he always had a problem himself in deciding what the pupil really meant. He was asked, 'How would you know if Nicholas was asking a *serious* question?'

6.5   T: It would depend on how he had been before he asked it. Because I do think that at times you know he wants to waste time and I'm not quite sure what reasons guide him, but he does like to attract a certain sort of attention to himself at times, whereas Stephen doesn't, and I have confidence, if you like, in Stephen's genuine inquiry, while Nicholas *may* be inquiring genuinely, but because of his past history I simply wouldn't know, so I think I'd go very much on what had happened in the lesson so far and perhaps his whole approach to me about it as well.

Stephen's seriousness provided a relatively constant context for interaction with the teacher, whereas encounters with Nicholas depended more on improvization and on *ad hoc* interpretations of his intent. The teacher often had difficulty therefore in understanding what Nicholas' questions meant. He found difficulty in creating a normal problem from what the boy said, and had to look carefully at the whole context of his behaviour to decide whether he was being serious or silly. In understanding, then, what pupils' problems were, the teachers had to look for evidence, using their spoken and written statements to create some form of pattern. Some of these patterns came to be seen as both persistent and general, like difficulties with reading. Some related to particular pupils — those, for example, who were lazy or who often asked silly questions. Some changed over time, with the diminishing difficulties of procedures of work. Other problems were generated by the course material currently in use, and here the teacher would have to use his knowledge of the learning which should be taking place to build up his picture of what the difficulty was. As we will see, this formulation of non-specific difficulties into specific problems is central to the process of solving those problems.

3 Generating Meanings

We turn now to look at two pieces of interaction with the same teacher in the same lesson. They illustrate the process outlined in the previous section, and they also illustrate how the pupil moves into the teacher's frame of reference by generating his own meanings from the clues provided by the teacher.

The first extract begins with the kind of detective work already described:

6.6 P: I don't understand that.
   T: You don't understand this — which bit?
   P: This.
   T: Which bit?
   P: Sir, this, where you have to sort it out.
   T: Do you understand this above it? ((The teacher then begins to go through the instructions.))

The pupil's statements are highly inexplicit, but the teacher infers that he has not understood the instructions properly and as the pupil does not contradict him he reads out the relevant passage(15):

> T: 'Pretend you are on a boat going to Tristan da Cunha. The boat lands on the beach. You are going to climb the mountain.' Right? Next, 'You will cross — you will cross these things. . . ((There is then a list which includes crater lake, stream, black beach, and cliff.)) Put them in the right order. Start with black beach.'

What the teacher does next is to elaborate on these written instructions. He continues:

> T: Now these aren't in the right order. What you have to say is which one would come first and which one would come after that, then after that and then after that, if you were going to climb the mountain. Where will you find the answer?
>
> P: Don't know.
>
> T: There. ((Pointing to the map of the island which showed the features mentioned in the question.)) And you will write them out and put them in the right order.

All of this is his elaboration of the written instruction, 'You will cross these things . . . Put them in the right order. Start with black beach.' What he is doing in the fine details of his talk is creatively linking the instructions with the task. The booklet does not actually say in as many words, 'Now these aren't in the right order.' The teacher says that so that it is clear. He translates the written instruction, 'Put them in the right order', into a form which incorporates the imaginary task of climbing the mountain, by saying, 'What you have to say is which one would come first, and which one would come after that . . . if you were going to climb the mountain.' This sentence is critical since it links the instruction with the imaginary task of climbing the mountain in a way that the text does not.

When the pupil indicates that he still does not understand, the teacher restates the task and then asks a further question — 'So that the thing you cross first would be . . . ?' — which is in the form he had created earlier, the form which incorporates the written instruction and the imaginary activity. The pupil's reply, 'Black beach', is taken as confirmation that he has got the point.

We therefore have a progression from the pupil's initially vague indication of *a* problem to the point where the teacher feels he has identified and remedied it. But of course he does not really know what the initial problem was. He can only restate the task, explicate it, make the instructions clearer, and hope that the pupil makes the necessary links. What he does take as clear is that the interaction has been successful, and he concludes it by saying, 'Well, I'm not going to tell you the answer, but you know how to find out now, right? Positive? Good lad, off you go.'

This example has concentrated on the teacher's side of the sequence, showing him listening to the pupil, creatively reinterpreting the instructions, and monitoring the pupil's replies. The next example shows a more active participation by the pupil in the generation of common meanings with the teacher. This conversation too was initiated by a pupil in trouble. He was stuck on the questions, 'Which side of the island . . . has most trees? Why?'

6.7   P: Sir, I don't understand. I've done the answer to that one, but then it says, 'Why?'
      T: Right, why's are always difficult, the difficult ones. Which side of the island, east or west, has most trees?
      P: The east.

This answer is correct, and we might guess that the pupil has found it out simply by looking at the map in his booklet, which showed trees growing on the eastern side. If he knows east from west, he can answer the question simply by looking. But the next question is not so easy. There are a few hints in the text about the importance of strong winds, but the pupil will have to draw on some knowledge from outside the curriculum. What the teacher does next is to provide some clues as to the kind of knowledge which might be involved. He is 'mapping' the problem itself, defining the area of search. Thus he says, 'Well, go on, what sort of things would decide where things grow?' This is a re-elaboration of the question 'Why?' which specifies that what needs to be considered in constructing an answer is information about soil conditions, climate, etc. There are many possible answers which the pupil could have provided from his commonsense knowledge, but he waits until he gets more guidance from the teacher about the *sort* of answer which is required. The teacher's elaboration of the written question shows him what information is likely to be relevant, and he then finds no difficulty in making suggestions. (16)

      T: Well, what sort of things would decide where things grow?
      P: Well, there's moisture and good soil.
      T: Moisture, good soil. What else?
      P: A bit of rain, sun.
      T: Well, rain would be part of moisture. Sun.
      P: Sun.
      T: There's one important thing you've left out.
      P: Growth.
      T: That's connected with the things you've just mentioned. But there's one important thing that you've left out.
      P: ((Silence.))

T: One important thing you've left out. ((He makes a movement with his hand to indicate a tree blowing in the wind.))

P: ((Silence.)) Sir, I don't know. ((Silence again.)) Sir, whether it's been planted.

T: Yeah, but you talked about that. It's really the sort of — um, if it's sheltered, if it's windy.

Once the pupil has been told to search around in his general knowledge for ideas about plant growth, he finds it easy to come up with some suggestions. But the teacher's non-commital responses indicate that something more is needed. When the pupil still fails to come up with the answer, he is told twice that he missed something 'important'. When even the strong visual clue is insufficient, there is a final more specific clue which indicates clearly the frame within which the answer is to be found.

T: . . . It's really the sort of — um, if it's sheltered, if it's windy. Now wind conditions are going to affect that, aren't they? How?

P: 'Cos if it is a strong hurricane it might blow it up, blow it down.

T: And if it is a cold wind, what might it do?

P: Freeze it and, um, it will die.

T: So it won't grow so well, will it?

What the teacher is doing is to supply a context within which the answer is located. He does so by providing a series of increasingly specific clues from which the child can elaborate his own meanings. The pupil draws on part of his general knowledge and integrates it into the framework of this particular problem. By indicating that one important factor affecting growth is wind conditions, the teacher has provided the pupil with a theme around which to document information from the written text and from his own general knowledge. Just as the teacher generates an understanding of the pupil's difficulties by interpreting what he says in terms of some pattern or conception of normal problems, so the pupil has to generate some pattern to fit the information the teacher is trying to communicate. In doing so he has to scan specific areas of his general knowledge as well as information in the booklet in order to try to make the same links between the two as the teacher obviously does.(17) As we saw he puts forward his answers in a tentative way and is ready to abandon them or lock in on them depending on whether or not they are confirmed by the teacher. Thus when the pupil says the cold will 'freeze it and, um, it will die', the teacher is able to take this as evidence that the pupil does now understand why trees do not grow on the west of Tristan. He hears this reply as evidence that the pupil has made the right links between the strong cold wind and the lack of trees. The pupil has (apparently) entered his system of meanings.

The implication of this analysis is that even where as in this example the search for the answer is closely guided, teachers can never actually *transmit* knowledge, for they are still dependent on the pupil undertaking his own interpretive work and making the necessary links for himself. Only by engaging in this essentially creative process can he enter the teacher's system of meanings. Only in this way can he learn.

4   Cumulative Curriculum Knowledge

Before we go on to look at resource-based learning in terms of this model two further points need to be made. We have suggested that behind this curriculum talk which we have been analysing lies a reciprocity of perspectives about, amongst other things, how teachers and pupils should behave and how classroom work is organized. This reciprocity of perspectives needs to be established and maintained as a prerequisite to curriculum talk. But it is also apparent that through the process of teaching, a reciprocity of perspectives is being established about academic meanings as well. Once the pupils have moved into the teacher's way of looking at a particular topic, this too can become part of the unspoken back-cloth of meaning to which they refer in order to understand what is being said. For example, one question in the booklet about Tristan da Cunha read, 'What colour is the sand on the beaches?' In discussing this question with a pupil, the teacher says:

6.8   T: What colour will the sand be?
      P: Black.
      T: Why?
      P: Sir, the volcanic ash.

The idea of volcanic ash had not been made explicit during this particular topic, but pupils had been told that the island was a volcano and they had previously learned about volcanoes. The written question therefore assumes the cumulative nature of the curriculum, requiring a piece of information which pupils are assumed to have learned earlier. They know what the question means because through earlier exposition they have developed a reciprocity of perspective with the teacher who set this question.(18)

One regular way in which teachers control cumulative subject meanings is by the use of a specialized language. Of course, as was pointed out earlier, not all the esoteric terms used by teachers are strictly needed in the sense that they do not all involve intellectual work.(19) Yet to the extent that a term makes some discrimination which is either not available to all, or is vaguer or more 'polluted' with everyday meanings in ordinary language — then the teacher cannot afford to tolerate apparent differences in meanings between himself and the pupils. He has to insist on *his* definition. Thus a reciprocity of meanings has to be established around each key term. The advantage of this definitional work for the teacher is that once a specialist meaning has been established he can talk with more precision to his pupils, because he knows that the term will summon up the same meanings in their minds as it does in his own.

Such terms also help to maintain the boundaries of different subjects, reminding the pupils *which* meanings it is appropriate to employ in this context. However, this process is easier to spot in some subjects than others. Physics teachers and chemists simply insist on the use of appropriate terms as part and parcel of their teaching. Of course, one of the difficulties of a subject such as Humanities is that there is no universal agreement about the meaning of many specialist terms. Nevertheless, they are still coined by teachers and help in maintaining a reciprocity of meanings. In the following example the teacher is introducing a term where there is general agreement about its meaning. A pupil had returned from the library room where he had gone to look up the term 'semi-detached'.

6.9   P: Sir, I know what it means now. Sir, two or more houses together, built together.

       T: Two or more?

       P: Yes.

       T: No. Semi-detached is two built together, if it's more what do they call them — when you've got a long row of houses built together? That's called terraced housing.

       P: Terraced?

       T: When you've got two, two together, that's a semi — a semi-detached.

       P: ((To friend.)) Doreen and our Nicky's is a semi-detached then, isn't it?

       Friend: Yes.

The pupil has been introduced to a new term and is actually able to reorganize some of his existing knowledge in the light of it ('Doreen and our Nicky's house . . .'). In the future the teacher will be able to use this term and know that it means the same to him as to the pupil.

Within a sophisticated curriculum package like MACOS, it is not surprising that there are quite specific specialist meanings which teachers try to communicate. One of the major areas of study in the section on the pre-literate Netsilik Eskimos was beliefs — the way in which they explained their world to themselves. Within the course, the notion of beliefs and explanations had particular functionalist overtones; they were seen as being used by people to help them get through life. In the following example it is apparent that the pupil too subscribes to this quite unusual notion of what beliefs are for. The question had read, 'How is it an advantage for the Netsilik to believe the seals allow themselves to be caught?'

6.10   T: Go on then, what do you think?
        P: Sir, if they don't catch them they don't think they've done it wrong.
        T: Mmm. What other ideas can you think of? It is quite a hard question, that, I think. ((Pause.)) Think about the time of the year and the difficulties of getting food. ((Pause.))
        P: Sir, sir, it would make them try harder.
        T: What will?
        P: It will make them try harder.
        T: Believing that seals allow themselves to be caught?
        P: Yes.
        T: Maybe it will, yes, maybe. There's another reason I can think of, though, which I think is more important. Is it easy or difficult to get seals at this time of the year?
        P: That time? Difficult.
        T: Yes. Now then, supposing that they go for days sometimes, they might go for days not managing to catch the seals. Now because they believe that seals allow themselves to be caught, it means that even if they go for days, they're going to think eventually they're bound to catch a seal because the seal will come to them and be caught. Right, so it's like a belief that keeps them going through a very difficult time.

Even though the girl did not get the answer quite right her attempt illustrates that she did understand the idea of beliefs correctly. Her suggestion that the Eskimos' belief would 'make them try harder' shows that she was at least on the same wavelength as the teacher. She had entered into this course's world of specialist meanings.

  We can now see that the words exchanged in curriculum talk not only depend on a background of organizational and relationship knowledge, but increasingly involve cumulative academic knowledge as well. By participating in a dialogue with their teachers, and by confronting the written curriculum, the pupils enter into a world of meanings some of which are specific to their own particular course of study and others related to the specialist subject as a whole. As in the case of organizational and relationship talk, these new academic meanings will soon disappear from the classroom transcripts. When they have been established they can be referred to in increasingly truncated ways, but once again they do not disappear from the interaction, they form an increasingly detailed background of meanings which teachers and pupils have to draw on together if they are to move on to the next topic of the curriculum.

Chapter 6: Notes and References

1   Cicourel *et al.* (1974), *Language Use and School Performance*. Cicourel notes: 'The basic issue here is that the participants must assume they are oriented to the "same" environment of objects despite cultural differences . . . If participants cannot make this assumption . . . then their interaction will become difficult at best' (p. 303).

2   The idea of a situationally embedded ignorance is not a new one and of course it is not *always* accepted by the pupils. Keddie (1971), 'Classroom Knowledge', in M. F. D. Young (ed.), *Knowledge and Control*, showed how some middle-class children more readily accepted that they were 'ignorant' than working-class children.

3   Cooper (1976), *Bernstein's Codes: A Classroom Study*, p. 15.

4   Barnes (1976), *From Communication to Curriculum*. Barnes has recently pointed out how little opportunity there is in most classrooms for pupils to relate their own out of school knowledge to the curriculum.

5   There are parallels here with experiments described by Garfinkel (1967), *Studies in Ethnomethodology*, where students were put in deliberately unusual situations. Like these pupils, Garfinkel's students would propose tentative interpretations of their situation and abandon them or lock in on them as *the* meaning of what was going on, depending on whether or not they were confirmed by what happened later.

6   For a discussion of teachers' control over what is to count as legitimate school knowledge, see Whitty and Young (1976), *Explorations in the Politics of School Knowledge*.

7   Garfinkel (1967), op. cit., defines the documentary method as follows: 'The method consists of treating an actual appearance as a "document of", as "pointing to", as "standing on behalf of" a presupposed underlying pattern. Not only is the underlying pattern derived from its individual documentary evidences, but the individual documentary evidences in their turn are interpreted on the basis of "what is known" about the underlying pattern. Each is used to elaborate the other' (p. 78).

8   Barnes (1976), op. cit.

9   Turner (1972), 'Some Formal Properties of Therapy Talk', in Sudnow, *Studies in Interaction*. There is a parallel here with Turner's description of group therapy sessions where the lay member is expected to offer a layman's version of his trouble and the expert transforms it into the language of the expertise involved (pp. 385–6).

10 For a sensitive analysis of how teachers type pupils see Hargreaves, Hestor, and Mellor (1976), *Deviance in Classrooms*.

11 Walker and Adelman (1972), *Towards a Sociography of Classrooms*, make a similar point.

12 Mehan (1974), 'Accomplishing Classroom Lessons', in Cicourel *et al.*, *Language Use and School Performance*. Mehan also describes the considerable degree of improvization contained in teachers' normal form definitions.

13 An analogy can be drawn here with Sudnow's (1965) account of a defending lawyer. The lawyer would interrupt his client as soon as he felt he had

enough information to 'confirm his sense of the case's typicality'. (Sudnow, 'Normal Crimes', *Social Problems* 12.)

14   Any two instances of reading difficulties are essentially different and seeing them as the same thing demands that we provide *ad hoc* grounds for their similarity. Garfinkel (1967), op. cit., shows that it is by this process of selectively viewing and continually reinterpreting and re-analysing events that we *create* the stable world that we think we inhabit.

15   The teacher does not hear the pupil as evading the question but asking legitimate questions as a preliminary to answering it. See Schegloff (1972), 'Notes on a Conversational Practice', in Sudnow (ed.), *Studies in Social Interaction*, pp. 78–9.

16   This is a very explicit example of what goes on all the time in normal conversations. Cicourel (1973), *Cognitive Sociology*, describes how 'Routine conversation depends upon speakers and hearers waiting for later utterances to decide what was uttered before'. This 'enables the speaker and hearer to maintain a sense of social structure despite deliberate or presumed vagueness' (p. 54).

17   Cicourel (1974), op. cit., explains how the ability to make such links is part of normal social competence: 'The hallmark of normal social competence is the reflexive linking of selectively attended information to what is stored in memory so that the emergent context can be handled routinely . . . The child must learn to fill in information from existing wholes or fragments and then retrospectively or prospectively to link the information to past and possible future objects or events' (p. 305).

18   As Cicourel (1974), op. cit., notes, 'The child must possess the ability to go beyond the information given and recognize that general appearances, utterances and gestures imply additional meanings' (p. 304).

19   Barnes *et al.* (1969), *Language, the Learner, and the School*.

Chapter 7
Varieties of Teaching

Introduction

The last chapter was directed to explicating a particular model of teaching and learning. Through the detailed analysis of teacher–pupil interaction, especially in the process of solving problems, we suggested that learning involved pupils in generating the same meanings for the curriculum material as their teacher subscribed to. In order to achieve that way of identifying and interpreting the facts, the pupils had to suspend any knowledge of the topic that they already had, at least provisionally, and generate new meanings within the frame of reference provided by the teacher. For his part, the teacher was seen as providing progressively more detailed clues about what meanings *were* relevant, and so as guiding and controlling the process of learning. Teachers and pupils were engaged in a sensitive interaction directed to the production of a mutual, and (as we will see later) often quite localized, meaning for the curriculum.

In the lessons which we recorded, a wide range of teaching methods were employed. Although the main medium was independent work on the various resources, there were also instances of different forms of class teaching. In the first part of this chapter, we will examine how these different forms and phases of class teaching were created through talk. From that analysis, we identify a similar structure in both class teaching and independent work. In both, the pupil has to step into the teacher's system of meanings, which either confirms or extends or even replaces his own. Increased control by pupils over the pacing of their work was not accompanied by any marked relaxation in the teachers' control over what was to count as knowledge.(1) What seemed to us to be involved was rather more a change in the technology of instruction than in the nature of learning.(2) This is not to deny, of course, that some technologies have advantages over others, and in the second part of the chapter we examine in terms of flexibility and control some of the advantages of resource-based learning.

1   Class Teaching

The teachers in this Humanities team often undertook formal class teaching at the beginning of a new topic, when their objective was to provide an introduction or an overview of what was to follow. They also used class teaching when they encountered some generalized difficulty; for example, we recorded whole lessons on how to construct a map from written instructions and on the interpretation of ancient myths about how the world began. At other times, teachers would call on everyone to pay attention for a few minutes while something was explained to everyone.

Class teaching can best be described as a process of 'telling'. The teacher is mainly concerned with communicating information — something he does less often (or at least less obviously) in resource-based learning — and he often manages a number of channels in the production of his message. He may lecture, elicit contributions from the pupils, use visual illustrations, or refer to a textbook, but whether his resources are simple or sophisticated, it is *his* talk which constitutes the lesson. He formulates what the textbook, the diagram, and even the pupils' contributions really mean, because he interprets their relevance to his theme. The use of the latest audio-visual equipment may get the message over more efficiently and the teacher who makes more use of pupils' ideas may be a better teacher(3), but these techniques do not change the underlying strategy, which is to 'tell' the pupil.

At the most simple level, the teacher can communicate his message by lecture. In most class teaching, though, at least with eleven-year-olds, there are few formal lectures. Far more common, as other researchers have described, is a procedure involving a combination of question and answers interspersed with brief periods of exposition, and the following example from early in the school year illustrates that pattern exactly.(4) It provides an excellent demonstration of how a teacher manages pupils' contributions in the production of a single message, and in this sense we argue that it is at root not very different from a lecture.

The knowledge base for the interaction which follows was a booklet on 'Myths of Creation'. The teacher had preceded the reading aloud of this material by explaining what 'creation' means, and what myths are for ('stories which help people to make sense of their world'). The facts were therefore given some preliminary framework within which they would make sense. He then invited pupils to contribute any myths they already knew, and when none were forthcoming, he claimed:

> We're all going to learn something here, then. None of us at the moment seems to know any myths about how the world began. At the end of the lesson, we'll all have learned something.

A great deal might be made of that 'we' as expressing a co-operative activity in which the teacher was included amongst the learners.(5) In the context of learning built around an official body of information, however, it is difficult to see it as more than a verbal gesture. At least on the surface, what is to be learned is determinate — so many facts about Sumerian and Chinese mythology. But, as we will see, the teacher's declared aim is that these facts shall be *understood*, and that a common sense of them is to be established. The difficulty of the task is announced at the outset:

> You know we think of people many years ago . . . We think the people were running around in bearskins and were a bit daft. But look what a complicated idea they've got here, as complicated an idea as we have. So let's see if we can work it out together.

In broad terms then, there was no doubt what this part of the lesson was about; pupils were not being left to work it out as they went along.(6)

Just before the interaction, which follows, the teacher had commented on the normal idea of God wanting the world to be a good place to live in.

7.1   T: Now then, it gets complicated now — 'God sent out two forces, Yin and Yang, to share his universe.' Well, first, what is 'universe'? What's the universe?

    P: The earth.

    T: Not just the earth, is it? What else?

    P: Everything.

    T: Yes, it's everything. So God has made this universe, God's made everything, and now there are these two forces Yin and Yang to control his universe. Two forces — how can we understand that? Anybody help us? Two forces — God sent out two forces. What does that mean? How can we get to that? What does the word 'force' mean?

    P: Two messengers who tell you what to do.

    T: Two messengers, that's one way we can think of it, yeah, good. That's some sort of idea, yeah.

    P: Sir, powers.

    T: Two powers — that's even better, isn't it, I think. So God sent out these two powers, and the Chinese called them Yin and Yang. But it's not easy for Yin and Yang — it's not easy for this earth, this universe, to be controlled by Yin and Yang because they're opposites. What's opposites? Somebody else have a go, we're getting the same people.

    P: Sir, enemies.

    T: OK, they don't necessarily have to be fighting all the time, but opposites are . . .

    P: Sir, different from each other.

    T: Different from each other, and when he says enemies, he's got the right idea. They're different from each other, and sometimes they're going to clash when they're opposites. OK, sometimes there's going to be trouble when they meet each other if they're opposites : : :

Sometimes they clash — it says here 'in conflict', that's what they mean, sometimes they're fighting. If you like, they're enemies — I think that's a good way of putting it : : : :

The content of the interaction is unusual, and so perhaps is the emphasis on getting to the meaning of the information, but its form is traditional. The teacher does most of the talking; he asks questions to which he clearly knows the answers, because he elaborates and evaluates the replies; and while those answers are never rejected as wrong (they are at worst 'some sort of idea'), they are absorbed into his developing exposition. Pupils' contributions are typically short; they seem to be made for instant elaboration, and they are fitted into the slots left by the teacher. The controlled allocation of terms is inseparable from the asymmetrical definition of meanings which are being shaped towards a common message. How is this common message achieved when there are so many participants? In the first place the teacher seems to know what meanings he wants to get at. He apparently knows what he wants to hear in the pupils' replies. He therefore either waits for the appropriate surface appearances of the theme he intends to develop or he elaborates (and if necessary translates) what is said into something he can use. He provides the framework into which pupil-talk is fitted, and grades it according to the closeness of fit.(7) Now this seems to us a sensitive piece of teaching if it is viewed from this perspective. Pupils' suggestions are not only accepted, they are incorporated in their *original form* into the teacher's account (*'God made everything'*, 'two *powers*', *'different from each other'*, *'enemies*, I think that's a good way of putting it'). But these pupils' suggestions are so abbreviated that their original meaning may well have undergone a considerable change in the course of their use. In managing the pupils' contributions in the production of a single message, the teacher selectively hears what they say and frequently translates it in a way to suit his own purposes. He chooses to assume that the pupils' utterances represent the same meanings as those *he* is pursuing and he spells out what they 'really' mean. As fellow teachers we can see the interaction as the 'managed product of one talker'.

What happens when the framing is relaxed a little? The extract quoted is untypical of the Humanities teaching in this school, most obviously in being *class* teaching. At this stage of the term, the syllabus was still being launched, and the teachers were doing more than their normal share of exposition to give pupils time to settle down. But even in the immediate context the interaction continued along rather different lines.

7.2   T: And what's the idea about the earth. Yin was the earth — 'dark, weak, cold, more like a woman' : : : : : What do you think? Do you agree with it?

Boy:	I do.
T:	You do — hang on — let's have a girl. Sylvia, come on, you seem to be willing to talk : : : :
P:	Rubbish.
T:	Rubbish. ((Laughter.)) Why is it rubbish? Or any of the girls, why do you think it's rubbish? What's it saying about women?
P:	They're weak.
T:	Right, yeah, it's saying that they're weak. Now would you agree?
Boy:	Yes sir.
T:	No, not the lads — that all women are weak.
Girls:	No, no, no.
Boys:	Yes, sir.
T:	Well, some of the boys think yes, all the girls obviously think no. Who do you think thought this myth up? Do you think it was a man or a woman?
All:	A man.
T:	Why do you say it was a man?
P:	'Cos he's saying horrible things about women.
T:	'Cos he's saying horrible things about women : : : : Well, I bet it was a man who first thought of it as well : : : : What do you think it would have been like for a woman living at that time? How do you think women were treated? From what's been said in the story so far, what do you think it would have been like?
P:	Terrible.
T:	Why do you think it would have been terrible?
P:	Because they had to work.
T:	They had to work, yes, I bet they did.
P:	They got whipped.
T:	They might have got whipped, they might have done, I don't know. And who's the gaffer? Who's in charge?
P:	The men.
P:	Stupid men. ((Laughter.))
T:	Stupid men, eh. ((Laughter.)) Right, *do you notice* what we've done? We started off saying we're going to look at ideas about the world, how people long ago explained the world. But what else — and this is very important — what else have we also done?
P:	Saw how men looked at women.
T:	We saw how men looked at women — you're nearly there. What exactly do you mean? Can you say — tell us a bit more, go on.
P:	How he doesn't like her, and how he thinks she's weak.
T:	Yeah. ((Tentatively.)) So we've also looked then — anybody else *before I say it,* anybody else have any ideas? He's on the right track there. He said that we've also looked at how man looked at woman. What else have we looked at here?
P:	God.
T:	No, not to do with God : : : :
P:	How they lived?

T: How they lived!! In other words the ideas they had about them-
        selves and how they lived. So from a story from long ago, we've
        used that story to work out how people thought about themselves,
        how they lived, as well as looking at their stories about the world
        we've used the stories to try to work out something about them.
        ((Interruption.)) Let's get on because this is *very* important,
        because all the time you're in Humanities you'll be doing this.
        You'll be looking at what people have said about themselves long
        ago, and trying to work out how they lived, and we call that
        something that you look for, *evidence*.

The teacher has here released some of his tight control over the
interaction in order to elicit more pupil participation; these are new
pupils, and most of them will need pushing into public talk. He does so
by trading on the normal taking of sides in the sex war, and inviting
opinions unpredictably related to his main themes. The first part is an
interlude which breaks the monotony of the previous teacher dominance, and is a preliminary to what *will emerge* as *having been* the main
purpose of the lesson. The teacher had earlier announced that the lesson
would be about how the Sumerians and Chinese invented myths to make
sense of the world, and he reminds them of this objective, but it now
appears that the lesson was really about other things as well, and pupils
were asked to reorient themselves within this larger framework of meanings.(8) This is achieved by a quite explicit series of metastatements,
talk about the talk, describing 'what we've done here'. Thus the lesson
involves a kind of counterpoint of messages with the second voice only
being recognized retrospectively. Yet both messages are the managed
product of the teacher. The first is achieved by commenting on, evaluating, and transforming pupil contributions so that they form part of the
emerging theme of the lesson, and the second by explicit metastatements
describing what has been done.(9) This is obviously a complex and
competent piece of teaching, yet however sophisticated it is we can still
see it as a variant of the lecture. The teacher is still trying to tell the pupils
something, and all his creativity is devoted to the production of these
messages.

Of course, not all class teaching can be described as a lecture or one of
its variants — teachers are not always involved in telling pupils things.
They sometimes want pupils to describe, to recap, they sometimes want
to test out what the pupils have learned, and they sometimes release their
control and allow pupils to take the initiative. Examples of each of these
different sub-phases occurred during lessons we recorded and each of
them could be seen to be managed by the teacher through his talk.(10)
As in the lecture he made statements about the sort of contributions the
pupils were to make, and he interpreted what they said in the light of

these instructions. In this way he controlled the pupils as they moved through different phases of lessons.

Our first example involves the pupils, with another teacher, in describing fossils that they had each been given. The teacher began this particular section of the lesson by making a series of statements outlining what the pupils were to do.(11)

7.3 T: Could anybody tell me what — sshh — tell me and tell the rest of us what you can see in the particular piece of stone that you've got? Put your hands up please and tell me. Yes?

   P: Sir, it's a shell.

   T: There's a shell in yours. OK. Anybody see anything else? Yes?

   P: Another shell.

   T: Another shell.

   P: Sir, shall we say how it got there?

   T: No, just tell me what you see first of all.

   P: Sir, it's all little, well, dead animals.

   T: Little dead animals. Right, that's a good description.

   P: Sir, mine's got all holes in it.

   T: Little holes in it, right. OK.

   P: Sir, it's like a snail's shell.

   T: It's like a snail's shell, yes, Susan.

   P: Sir, mine's got lines on it.

   T: Lines, right, OK. Anything else?

   P: Mine's got part of a shell that's been carved on it.

   T: A shell that's been carved. All right.

   P: Sir, this has as well.

Not only does the teacher instigate this transaction by explicit instructions, he also selectively listens and evaluates what they say in terms of these instructions — one response is heard as a 'good description' and the offer to 'say how it got there' is rejected as premature. In this way the teacher can carefully control the way the pupils participate in his lesson.

Another sub-phase within the class lessons involved a recap; the teacher was trying to reintroduce very specific ideas that had emerged earlier in the day. During the lesson on the myths of creation, it had become apparent that many of the pupils did not know where the rivers Tigris and Euphrates were — indeed many of them did not know where Africa was. The teacher announced his intention to 'have a special lesson when we bring down a globe and *show* you these places.' That afternoon he took twelve girls from his own group (the largest number that could easily see the globe at one time) to a corner of the open area while the rest of the double class carried on with their own work under his colleague's supervision. This is how the session began:

7.4   T: Right, now, why did we say we brought this down? What was the problem we had this morning?

P: Africa.

T: Well, what was it about Africa? What weren't we sure about?

P: Where Africa is.

T: Right, one was where Africa is — and something else we were asking ourselves. Yeah?

P: We were asking where the two rivers were.

T: Yeah. Anybody remember the name of these two rivers?

P: Nile.

T: Nile was one that was mentioned.

P: Euphrates.

T: Euphrates, great. What was the name of the other one?

P: Tigris.

T: Smashing, right. Tigris and Euphrates.

Like many of the examples of problem-solving quoted in the previous chapter, this is a question-and-answer routine. But it has very different functions. The teacher apparently has something quite specific in mind. He wants to get quickly to the point where certain ideas are reintroduced to the group so that he can tie this lesson to the previous one. He knows precisely what answers he wants. The first 'wrong' answer — 'Africa' — is used to reformulate the question in a way which gives a further clue about what he is after. By progressively commenting on and evaluating replies and revising his questions, the teacher finally manages the answer he requires. All he has asked the pupils to do is to search their memories for the correct pieces of information to fill the gaps in the 'story' he is going to tell. They are not asked to *use* that information, nor is it necessary for them all to remember it. The teacher only needs one person to tell him for the idea to be reintroduced. The same pedagogic end could have been served if he had simply told the pupils in the first place where the two rivers were. But by his questions, he has involved the pupils themselves in the process of telling. The sequence also illustrates the cumulative nature of school knowledge; this morning's lesson topic has become this afternoon's common knowledge.

The purpose of locating these rivers was to *see* where 'men first started to farm'. The next phase of the lesson was a natural development from this; it is more like a lecture since it involves telling the pupils something new.

7.5   T: Anybody any idea why farming should begin there? What do you need to farm?

P: Soil

P: Water.

T: Good soil, good water. What else do you need?

P: Animals.

T: Not animals straightaway.
P: Seeds, sir.
T: Seeds, good thinking. Do you know — where did wheat come from and barley that we know now? Did somebody wake up and, say, 'Right, I'm going to invent wheat.' How could you do that? Where could you get it from? ((Pause.)) Where do you think it comes from — what's it look like?
P: Corn.
T: That's right, a sort of corn.
P: Sir, Ethiopia hasn't got no food.
T: Well, no, parts of it — you're right. But keep to this one — where do you think wheat came from? How do you think they found out about it? . . . Any ideas? . . . In this part of the world it grew naturally — a type of wheat grew naturally and people found they could use it to make bread . . .

In this sequence, the initial question is followed immediately by a further question — 'What do you need to farm?' — which indicates what kind of answer is required. From there on, the teacher is listening for the sort of replies that can feed into his theme. He knows what he wants to get across about wheat, and he is again trying to integrate the pupils into that 'telling' process. The comment about Ethiopia is not taken up because of its irrelevance to the theme. In the end, because no one provides his answer, the teacher has to tell the group that 'a type of wheat grew naturally and people found that they could use it to make bread'. His reiterated request for 'any ideas' did not in fact mean *any* ideas, but only those which could be used for the purpose of the moment. His talk is full of 'transaction pauses' — implicit invitations for pupils to butt in — but when they fail to do so he has to tell the 'story' himself.(12) As we have already argued, this is very different from the questioning and answering that goes on when the teacher is problem-solving. Then it is essential that the *pupils* have or acquire the appropriate meanings. But here the teacher is looking for answers which he can integrate into his own theme.

After the talk about wheat, and about the beginning of farming in the Middle East, the teacher went on to ask the group how they would get to the Middle East.

7.6 T: . . . I wonder if anybody knows what it is called from the Mediterranean and the Red Sea?
P: Suez.
T: Oh! Oh! (('Applause' for a girl consistently successful in her answers on this occasion.)) Yes, and you go through that canal to the Red Sea and come round to the Persian Gulf.
P: Sir, where's Germany on that?
T: Germany? There. France — look, Germany's next door to France.

P: My brother's in Germany.
T: Is he? Is he in the army?
P: Don't know sir.
T: Ah, right.
P: Hey, sir, my uncle's in the army.
T: Is he abroad as well?
P: He was in the Bahamas. He's home now.
T: The Bahamas — it's nice and sunny there, isn't it?
P: He took his wife and kids with him.
T: Yeah. OK, any more questions about *this*?

At this stage of the interaction, the teacher had finished 'lecturing', at least for the moment, and so (unlike the earlier comment about Ethiopia) he did not hear the topic change by the pupils as deviant. These girls seemed to have recognized that the teacher had 'finished', and so went on to take the initiative themselves. The teacher is prepared to *follow* them, hearing their questions as legitimate in a way that he would have been unable to do if he had wanted to pursue his theme further. In other words, his notion of what the lesson is about has changed, and he is willing to hear pupils' questions as legitimate requests for information and not as deviant (or at least inappropriate) attempts to change the topic. The lecture model is no longer appropriate and what we have is a 'side-sequence' from the main topic.(13) Once again, of course, it is instigated, and, as we will see, concluded, by the way the teacher hears and comments on what the pupils say.

The lesson was concluded by the teacher checking on what had been learned. In this checking phase, the replies of a few pupils seemed to be taken as evidence that the whole group had 'got the idea', and the very brief answers were filled out by the teacher. As usual in class teaching, the evidence on which the teacher depends to tell him if pupils have understood is highly circumstantial.

7.7   T: Yeah. OK any more questions about *this* 'cos I want the lads to — oh, it's ten past now : : : : Right, well, we'll show the lads tomorrow perhaps. Any more questions about that before we go back? ((Silence.)) No? ((Silence.)) What's the hottest part of the world, did we say, somebody mentioned it?
P: The equator.
T: The equator, yeah. What are the continents? Anybody remember?
P: Australia, America.
T: America, Africa.
P: Africa, Asia.
T: Yeah, Asia, Africa . . .

In this final section the teacher appears to be hearing the pupils' replies as evidence that they have absorbed what he has been telling them during the lesson. Unlike earlier question-and-answer sessions he now takes the fact that a *few* of them can mention *some* of the continents as evidence that they have *all* got the idea. He fills in what the one-word answer 'Australia' really means and takes it as evidence that all the pupils have understood what he has been telling them.

Although the main business of class teaching is telling, and even the checking phase functions as a re-telling, we have seen how teacher and pupils talk and listen to each other in a variety of ways at different stages in their interaction. We have identified an introductory phase where the teacher was simply trying to elicit *the* ideas of an earlier lesson, those that were relevant to his present concerns. There was a central 'lecture' phase, where the teacher's main purpose was exposition but where he also involved pupils in the telling. There was a 'side-sequence' where he relaxed his control over the topic, and allowed pupils to instigate their own search for information. Finally, there was a checking phase where he heard the replies of a few pupils as evidence that they had all got the point. The teacher controls these different phases largely by listening and responding to pupils' talk in different ways.

These varieties of class teaching may seem quite different from the resource-based learning from which examples were drawn in the previous chapter, and to which we return in the following section. But we would argue that these differences represent a change only in surface structure, in the technology of putting the facts across, while the underlying process of learning remains essentially the same.

The following example illustrates our point. The teacher had drawn the outline of an island on the overhead projector, and was now adding other features. He did so by calling for information from pupils.

7.8   P: Sir, it says the plain stretches from the south-east to the north-west of the island.

T: All right, so we know that the plain extends from south-east to north-west. In other words, the plain — who shall I pick, who shall I pick? — Stephen, come and show people on the map where you think we're going to find the plain, If it's going from south-east to north-west . . . ((Stephen moves over to the overhead projector.)) There you are — on there. Point to where the plain will be.

P: Where has it got to be?

T: South-east to north-west. ((Pause.))

P2:   Come on, Steve.

T: Shut up, Michael. ((Pause.)) Point to south-east on the map.

P: Sir, there?

T: OK, south-east. Where's north-west? Everybody check as he points on the map — you can see it on the board. Now, where's north-west? ((Stephen points.)) Good, so where is the plain going to run from then? ((Pause.)) So it goes from south-east to north-west. So where's it going to go on the map?

P: In the middle.

T: Where do you mean, in the middle? Point to where you mean. ((Stephen points to the middle.)) Well, that's not south-east to north-west, is it?

P: ((Quietly.)) No.

T: Can somebody help Steve? We've got a problem. It says the plain runs from south-east to north-west? Go on, Lorraine.

P: Sir, it goes from the south-east and stretches up to the north-west.

T: Yeah, it *stretches* from the south-east of the island to the north-west. Go on then, Steve, it stretches from the south-east to the north-west.

P: Is it up there?

T: It is up there, where else is it as well?

P: Er . . .

T: It's got to stretch from south-east to north-west — make it *stretch*.

P: Sir, draw a dirty big line up there? ((Teacher agrees and lets him draw a line, but he later indicates that the line is not really correct.))

As in the individualized problem-solving encounters examined in the previous chapter, we can see the pupil trying to move towards the teacher's understanding of what the task involves. He makes several tentative suggestions, but when it becomes apparent that he does *not* understand, he falls silent. There is some help from another pupil, but it is the teacher's instruction to 'make it stretch' that allows him partly to complete the task. This is an unusual example because the teacher is using a pupil as one of his resources in the exposition. Because that pupil's difficulties become apparent, they get put into words and so form part of the message of the lesson. It can be argued that the other fifty pupils observing this demonstration are going through a similar process of generating meanings within the framework provided by the teacher, but they have to do it in their heads. When he is class teaching, the teacher can actively involve very few pupils. He can use various checking procedures, but inevitably he must take a few right answers as evidence that his immediate purposes have been achieved. Most of the interpretive work being done by pupils therefore remains hidden. Resource-based learning may not be, in its deep structure, any more open. But as practised in this school, it allows more sensitivity to pupils' acquisition of the teacher's meaning. It is to this greater sensitivity that our analysis now turns.

2   Advantages of Resource-Based Teaching

Research techniques inevitably limit the scope of any analysis. Concentration on the teacher's talk, whether to groups or individual pupils, was a powerful constraint on our investigation of resource-based teaching. This style of teaching is designed to allow pupils to work largely on their own. They would therefore initiate contact with the teacher only when they had problems, and we have seen that problem-solving becomes the teacher's major function in this context. We do *not* know what happens when things go right for them. There was obviously a great deal more talk going on than ever found its way on to our tapes. Some of the conversation between pupils was inevitably just chatter, but a large amount of it appeared to be work-directed. Pupils would talk over their problems, argue about possible interpretations, and discuss points arising out of the curriculum material. Unfortunately, the technical problems of capturing any of this pupil-talk without disrupting the lesson proved insurmountable, and after some dismal trials we decided to concentrate on the teacher. Our view of resource-based teaching is therefore very one-sided. As a retrospective justification, we might argue of course that when pupils are working 'successfully', their reasoning does not always get into words anyway. They talk about their work most explicitly when they get into difficulties, or when demonstrating to a friend how to do it. Recording them apart from the teacher would not necessarily have guaranteed a fuller picture of what was going on inside their heads.

From the recordings we do have, certain distinctive features of this kind of teaching seemed to emerge quite clearly. We are tempted to call them advantages, but will limit our account (at least overtly) to description. We consider two of these features in detail because we have most information about them, but two other characteristics will be mentioned briefly.

The process of learning appears more active than in traditional teaching. Pupils continually have to read material through, and to answer questions which require them to engage directly with the subject content. In the last example, the pupil drawing a plain onto a map made it clear that he had not understood the teacher's comment that the plain extended from one side of the island to the other. His difficulty is shown up because *he* is picked on to do the collective job, but the rest of the class may have had the same or related difficulties which remained hidden. If the task had confronted *each* of them, they would have had to engage actively with the problem of how a plain extends over an area, and would not have been able to leave most of the work to the teacher. This is not to deny, of course, that conventional class teaching can also involve a great deal of practical work. But in the classroom we observed, it was the main constituent.

Because this was so, pupils could pace their own work. With class teaching, the teacher has to set a common pace. It was fortunate for Stephen that the teacher chose him as guinea-pig, and so brought his difficulty into the open. That difficulty then became a common problem — 'We've got a problem' — and the lesson slowed to his pace. In working creatively to remove that difficulty, the teacher was establishing 'the' answer for the entire group. But for many pupils (for example, Lorraine) who already knew the answer, the pace was too slow. For some others who were silent, it may still have been too fast. We referred earlier to assuming what should be taught, and teaching what could be assumed. In class teaching, these 'errors' are endemic. In problem-solving exchanges with individual pupils, there is more opportunity to establish *what*, and *how much*, needs to be said.

The necessity for pupils to take an active part in their learning, and the opportunity to pace their work for themselves, are frequently cited as characteristics of resource-based learning. In the rest of this chapter, we examine features which are perhaps less obvious but which became particularly apparent because of the model of learning which we developed from studying the transcripts. We characterize these in terms of flexibility and control.

Confronting a whole class, the teacher has to use necessarily sketchy evidence to determine the level at which to pitch his exposition. By asking occasional questions and interpreting looks of puzzlement, interest, or boredom, he has to guess whether or not the class is following him. Even when he is experienced in such monitoring and is teaching in a streamed school, a uniform response is very unlikely. With mixed-ability classes, it is an impossibility.

Differences in the pace and level of work are partly catered for in the Humanities teaching we observed by the production of booklets intended to vary in difficulty. But this was only a preliminary provision. Being largely freed from the business of telling, the teachers were able to spend most of their time with individual pupils, and this made possible a considerable flexibility in treatment. In the way he handled their queries and problems, a teacher could create localized meanings with his pupils; in a sense he could create different curricula for individual pupils.

We have already seen that when a teacher works with an individual pupil, he frequently tailors his explanation of the problem to include or reformulate points mentioned by that pupil. Even in the map-drawing lesson, the teacher continually rephrased his questions in a way that would help the pupil to follow, and so his exposition was at least partly an improvization. Working more intensively with a single child, and without the audience of fifty others, he would have more chance to establish where the pupil was in that particular problem and to adapt his teaching accordingly. The example which follows involves a girl working on the easier booklet on Tristan da Cunha.

7.9   T: Right, I'll read to there and then you read that. 'Tristan da Cuhna is an island where about 300 people live. Why are we learning about Tristan da Cuhna? A group of people who live together are called a community.' . . . What's a community?

P: ((Mumbles.))

T: What's a community?

P: Er . . . ((Silence.))

T: Were you listening? ((Pause.)) You weren't? ((Laughs.)) ((He reads the passage again.)) So what's a community?

P: A group of people . . .

T: Who . . .

P: That live on the island there, er, three years ago.

T: Well, it's a group of people who live together. So a community is a group of people who live together. Right? What's a community?

P: When people live together.

T: A *group*.

P: A group of people who live together.

T: That's right. It could be any group of people, not just Tristan but any group of people who live together — we call that a community.

The purpose of this exchange is to get the pupil to repeat the definition of a community. The teacher may not have set out to teach that definition in such a narrow, repetitive way, and we might guess that his initial request that she repeat what he had just said was a check on her attention. But when she fails to do so, even when he has read the text again, getting her to repeat the definition becomes the main task of the moment. It is only when she *is* able to say the words that he goes on to expand on the definition and to emphasize its applicability to any group living together. The appearance of an apparently basic difficulty in comprehension forced him to narrow the curriculum to a simple repetition of the facts.

Unlike the class teaching we described earlier, the teacher is not engaged in producing a common message — he works creatively with the written curriculum and the pupil in the production of quite *localized* meanings. Together they produce something that is acceptable to the teacher as some sort of work, but which is in fact quite specific to a particular child in terms of what he knows about her as an individual — her ability, her level of reading, and her past knowledge, etc. Once the girl had got over this initial difficulty she managed (with some assistance) to read the passage in the booklet and to tackle some simple questions. During the lesson she went up to the teacher four more times, at five-minute intervals. Each time she was stuck on something different and each time he was able to reorient himself to her as an individual and work with her in the production of some sort of common understanding of what the question wanted. In formulating problems and in mapping the area of search for the answer, the teacher was able to be sensitive to her as an individual and create a curriculum appropriate to his conception of what she needed.(14)

Evidence of teachers narrowing down the curriculum must be matched by evidence of its expansion to allow greater freedom to other pupils. In the example which follows, the teacher explicitly divests himself of the role of authority on the topic in hand, and the topic itself was not 'authorized' by the curriculum.

7.10 P: Sir, how fast does the world travel round and round?
      P: 3,600 miles an hour, sir.
      T: Is it? I don't know.
      P: What?
      T: I don't know. Do you want to go and look it up in the encyclopedia?
      P: Yes, sir.
      T: Look it up.
      P: The world, what do you look up for — the world? ((Teacher and pupils go off to the library room.))
      P: Earth.
      T: Here's the earth, the book on the earth, take that out. Take it out if you like and see if you can find it in there, lads. ((They return to the classroom.))

The initial question was off the official point, but as the teacher explained later, the pupils were so interested in what they were discussing that he did not want to discourage them. Later that week, problems occurred *within* the framework of the official topic — one on the size of an albatross and one on the meaning of 'semi-detached'—and the same two pupils volunteered to look the facts up for themselves. Although they were using only the small Humanities library, second-year pupils were sometimes sent off to the main library of the Community Centre. In this way, teachers were able to expand the curriculum for those who worked fast or who showed a special interest in some aspect of their work. The increased time available for contact with individual pupils made this flexibility far more possible than in normal class teaching.

In their forward planning, the Humanities team were constantly re-evaluating the quality of the written material which they were using. In the complex business of setting up resource-based learning in a new school, some of the early material had inevitably been prepared hurriedly, and some of the tasks which pupils were set involved the kind of closely prescribed exercises which are the staple diet of so much worksheet teaching. There was a general concern in the team to replace the narrower activities with a more demanding curriculum. The introduction of MACOS had been one main attempt to do this. It was seen as a more sophisticated approach to learning because it involved pupils in a great deal of cognitive work. But again, the teachers were not yet satisfied with the booklets they had constructed and were aware that some of the concepts to be achieved by pupils had been reduced to facts to be taught like anything else.(15) Nevertheless, when the second-year course was working properly, it produced some striking evidence of pupils having to generate new conceptual frameworks and to accommodate existing knowledge within them.

Once again, the underlying nature of the curriculum is revealed in the type of talk which pupils and teachers engage in during the solving of problems. The lesson illustrated below was recorded early in the year. The key concept to be put over was the notion that animals can be seen to have adapted their bodily structures to help them fit into their particular environment. There had been a lead lesson on this topic, and pupils were now working alone or in pairs prior to seeing a film on the life of the salmon. The teacher was helping a pupil in difficulties:

7.11   T: Now the structure of the elephant that's picked out is the long trunk, right? How does the trunk help the elephant behave? It can pick up food with it, right, and squirt water over itself and wash itself. So if you said your tongue, your short tongue — now how does that structure, your short tongue, help you behave?

        P: To talk, to eat.

        T: Right, right, you've got the idea, haven't you? Well, you've picked out the tongue, what does that help the frog do?

        P: Eat.

        T: Right.

In this example, the teacher is working with an abstract concept about the relationship between bodily structures and the function they serve. What he and the booklet are trying to achieve is to get the pupil to use that concept to look at different animals and their structures. Yet the teacher does not put this idea into words — he achieves it by example. When he says, 'Right, you've got the idea', he presumably has heard her reply ('To talk, to eat') as evidence that she understands. He hears her as understanding the relationship between structure and function in the same way as he does, and as being able to place existing knowledge in that new framework.

This reworking of existing knowledge is made apparent in the following extract from the same lesson. Once again the teacher is trying to get the pupils to place something they already know into a new framework but he fails because they do not have the requisite facts to start with.

7.12 P: What do you write there?
       T: Ah, this one. OK — right, see these — we've got nine animals here
           : : : : Pick five of them. Elephant — long trunk. Now pick one other
           of those, pick any one.
       P: Whale.
       T: All right, pick one of the structures of the whale.
       P: Its teeth.
       T: Right, its teeth. And how do its teeth help it to survive — what can it
           do with its teeth?
       P: Bite people.
       T: Well, whales don't eat people — what do they eat?
       P: Fish.
       T: Actually they don't eat fish — no, even smaller than fish, whales eat.
       P: Crabs.
       T: No, they don't eat crabs.
       P: Snails.
       T: No, its another word that you might not have heard of. Have you
           heard of the word — a-l-g-a-e?
       P: No, I won't pick that one, I'll pick another one.
       T: All right, give me a structure. ((Pause.))
       P: Duck.
       T: Er, wait a minute, give me a structure on the body of that animal.
       P: Feather.
       T: All right. How does the feather help it behave?
       P: Keeps it warm.
       T: That'll do — you get 'duck — feather — helps to keep it warm'.

Once again, the teacher is listening to what pupils say for evidence that
they have got the idea. He wants to know if they can *use* the idea of a
relationship between structure and function by applying it to a number
of different animals. Both he and the text are therefore assuming the
existence of some common knowledge (e.g. that whales eat algae) which
can be reorganized. When these necessary facts are *not* available, then
more conventional exposition becomes necessary. Recognizing his lack
of the necessary knowledge resources, it is not surprising that this pupil
decides that he 'won't pick that one'.

MACOS was originally designed for class teaching and translating
into a form suitable for individualized learning has been a difficult
business. Yet this translation has made possible a much greater control
over what is actually taught. However well planned a curriculum may be
at the general level, what is important is the work pupils carry out when
they engage with the material. MACOS is an attempt to introduce a
certain sort of conceptual work to the classroom and this denotes a
certain sort of questioning, for as we have seen it is the questions and
answers as defined by the pupils or the teachers and pupils together
which constitute the child's experience of the curriculum. If MACOS is

to achieve the sort of conceptual work it aspires to and not deteriorate to a simple transmission of facts (a criticism often levelled at Nuffield Science) then considerable care and attention need to be devoted to what the pupils are asked to do in their questions and answers. Writing the material down, and carefully re-evaluating it in the light of experience, as these teachers did, obviously increases their control over what the pupils take from their courses. In other words they can monitor and more effectively evaluate what they are teaching.

The production of written course guides therefore forces teachers to be much more explicit about what they want to teach. But such explicitness has a double edge, for as these teachers were beginning to find, once they have been explicit, their scope for future manoeuvre becomes limited. And it is limited not only by the course material but also by the pressures within the team for common teaching strategies. Bernstein has suggested that integrated curricula tend to create homogeneity in teaching practice, because teachers have to work closely together if they are to subordinate previously separate contents to some relational idea, and because in their teaching they will become unusually visible to one another.(16) But as we noted in Chapter 4, a consistent reconciliation of possibly diverse strategies requires certain structural conditions to be met, such as a commitment to integrated studies as something more than a marginal addition to normal subject responsibilities, and the possibility of regular formal and informal contacts between team members. In the context we have described, there seemed to be a considerable sense of common purpose and common practice. This does not mean, however, that the teachers felt that they had arrived, even for the time being, at their pedagogical destination.

We have noted their departure from the practice of 'standing up there and spouting, and telling everyone what to do', and their search for other ways of learning than 'responding to authority in the front of the class'. Yet their abandonment of traditional teaching strategies occasionally worried them when they reflected on their transformation from being resources of information to being resources of where to find it. The dilemma is best expressed in their own words.(17)

> You are no longer *the* prime source of authority because the kids are increasingly coming in and organizing themselves. But a slightly detrimental effect, I think, is that the teacher in some ways isn't valued as highly as a source either of information or inspiration, because you can tend to become an adjunct of booklets. On the authority side, I think it's a good thing that they come to regard you as an additional source rather than the only source. But it can become slightly undemanding.
>
> I think there's an amusing side to that, it's that we're no longer resources

> of information, we're resources of where to find information. In other words, they don't say to us, 'How is this sledge made?', they say, 'Where's the booklet that tells us how to make a sledge?'

The resulting new role was still very demanding and we have tried to show some of the varied problem-solving in which the diagnosis and treatment of individual difficulties had room to be more subtle than is normally possible with whole-class teaching. But there was a certain monotony in the repertoire of basic teacher performances. Whole lessons devoted to class teaching were rare, much more frequent were brief interruptions by the teacher, when 'there's something you think you've forgotten or haven't realized is going to be a problem'. These interruptions were sometimes regarded as just that by the pupils:

> You know, they've said to me, 'We want to get on with our work, don't stand there talking, we want to get on with our work.'

> That's exactly what I mean, though, about the undervaluing of the teacher. Because we *do* have a lot to offer, and the kids don't realize it.

In many of the lessons we observed, a high work-rate seemed to be achieved with little coercive pressure from the teacher. The sequential nature of the course guides seemed to develop its own momentum. It seemed to one of the team to 'introduce a sort of competitive element' so that their urge to get on could make pupils impatient with any intrusion of irrelevant material. There is undoubtedly a danger in resource-based learning that the process becomes mechanized, and these teachers were aware of it. They were also becoming worried about the infrequency of activities involving whole groups of children together, and their plans for the following year were beginning to include provision for more discussion and even for more teacher exposition (and inspiration). The team co-ordinator expressed his 'revisionism' in this way:

> One thing I've found in my time here is that when I first came I removed myself as far as possible from being a source of authority, because I thought everything had to be the kids on their own. And increasingly I've come to realize that the teacher is necessary at certain points because the kids can't necessarily grasp things as thoroughly as we'd like. I've come to regard the [teacher's] role more highly than I did when I first came. I don't know if that's the weakness of the materials we've produced, or just the fact that certain things do need a teacher to reinforce them. I tend to think it's the latter.

These doubts indicate the possibility of at least tactical changes within the strategic commitment to reducing the overt dominance of the teacher. Of course such changes would need the agreement of the *team*, but if they agreed then what we have referred to repeatedly as organizational constraints would allow considerable diversity. What strikes us most forcefully as observers, though, is that this diversity of approach is mainly superficial. We argued earlier that resource-based learning has involved a change in the technology of teaching rather than a basic departure from the transmission of knowledge, and in the next chapter we offer a structural analysis of the uniformities underlying these varieties of teaching.

In resource-based teaching, the structure of the learning is provided by the course guides. Direct dependence on the teacher at each stage of acquiring the relevant material is therefore reduced. It becomes possible for pupils to feel more in control of what they do, because they can see for themselves what is (and will be) going on, and because they gradually learn to take over longer and longer stretches of their work. The resulting sense of social responsibility is seen in the school as reducing discipline problems. Breaking up the single verbal encounter which is still so prevalent in secondary schools has certainly reduced the number of occasions for minor deviance, and so avoided the endless confrontations likely where teachers are constantly defending the integrity of that encounter. It also allows pupils to work at their own pace, and at tasks of which the immediate and long-term purpose has been explained. But greater control over the pace of transmission must be distinguished from control over the actual meanings being transmitted. Bernstein has argued that integrated curricula reflect different conceptions of social order from those expressed in conventional subject divisions. In the latter, the learner is necessarily treated as being ignorant of the matters in hand, everyday knowledge having to be carefully screened before its relevance to classroom learning can be admitted. The purpose even of particular lessons may be left so unclear as to increase dependence on the teacher, while in relation to the long-term process of transmission the learner has 'little status and few rights'.(18)

Integrated curricula are likely to emphasize ways of knowing rather than states of knowledge. If these ways are made available to the pupil early in his learning career, then his control over at least the pace of learning is increased and his helplessness in the face of didactic teaching is reduced. But pupils' existing knowledge is not necessarily admitted any more freely. Bernstein comments that without consensus and clarity about the ideas which integrate 'previously insulated subjects', the learning which results may be so open that 'neither staff nor pupils have a sense of place, time or purpose'.(19) This openness by default was not apparent in the teaching we observed. The original courses on which much of the Humanities teaching was based had been built on a clearly defined conceptual structure. In freely adapting them to a particular

context, past and present members of the Humanities team had both
added new material, some of it relating to the local community, and
made extensive changes in methods of transmission. The evident blurring of boundaries between 'previously insulated subjects' had not led to
a similar blurring of boundaries between the knowledge contained in the
course guides and 'the everday community knowledge of teacher or
taught'. Bernstein's whole analysis accepts the possibility that integration may take place without greatly increasing pupils' control over what
they learn or how they learn it, but it also points to the likelihood that the
reduced discretion of teachers will be 'paralleled by an increased discretion of the pupils . . . there is a shift in the balance of power'. Our own
account suggests the need to be clear about the kind of discretion which
the pupils have obtained. If they work mainly from resources rather than
from information provided by the teacher, then they are less obviously
'doing the teacher's work'. They no longer have to work at a common
pace, and they can often choose whether or not to enter directly into
interaction with the teacher. But the knowledge being transmitted has
been carefully packaged, structured, and reinforced. They are still moving into the teacher's meaning system and leaving it relatively undisturbed.

This very limited discretion, involving control over the pace of learning rather than over the knowledge itself, has to be seen in the larger
context of a *gradual* training in independent study. What is done in the
Lower School can only be a preliminary stage; in this sense, the whole
two years might be seen as a period of settling in. When we described in
Chapter 5 the closely prescribed tasks given to the children in their first
lessons in Humanities, we described them as part of a holding operation
which freed the teachers for the tasks of establishing working procedures
and dealing with urgent difficulties. But we also cited some examples of
rather different working methods being explicitly announced — for
example, that what mattered was not the fact but the pupil's own search
for it. We conclude this chapter by looking at two instances where the
teacher's control over meaning was relaxed, and where increased pupil
discretion is perhaps apparent in the text. The first example occurred
early in the first year. Two boys were discussing the end of the world. It
was off the subject, but they were very involved in it and the teacher left
them to carry on. Eventually they drew him into the discussion too.

7.13   P1: Yeah, and say the Americans are getting beat, couldn't they just press
          a button and this bomb goes off and explodes the world.
       T: Oh, the Americans can destroy the world many times over.
       P1: And you know what, they've got houses like . . . and when the bomb

> goes off they can go down underground : : : ((Largely untranscrib-
> able, but about what these houses are like.))

T: Well, what, er, what would be the point of blowing up the world and having to live below the ground?

P2: Yeah.

P1: No, this is like — sir, they don't want — if they're getting beat, and getting blowed up, and then they go down and everyone dies, and when they come up they'll be all right, won't they?

P2: Well, what's the use of them living on the earth all on their own?

T: No, couldn't happen, because if you had an atomic war — have you heard of radiation?

P1: Yeah.

T: Well, the point is that radiation hangs around for years and years killing people.

P1: Well, er . . .

T: So what's the point in blowing up everybody?

P1: Yeah, but, er, when all that blows away, then they just come up again.

This discussion — and it *is* a discussion, not a lesson — is very different from normal classroom talk. Both pupil and teacher have access to facts. One knows about the bomb and the fall-out shelter. The other accepts these as facts, but advances new facts (about radiation) to advance his argument. The pupil, however, stands by his position. We might suggest that in a normal teaching situation, the exchange would have ended like this:

T: So what's the point of blowing up everybody?

P: None, because no one would survive.

T: Good, that's right.

This was *not* the ending, because there was no compelling reason for a common meaning to emerge. Indeed, in reading this piece of interaction, we do not have to invoke the notion of hierarchy, or of the teacher owning the talk. If the identifying labels were removed, it would not be easy to identify the teacher at all. He neither begins nor ends the exchange, he does not allocate turns, and he *responds* to what the pupils say rather than evaluating it. In terms of our own earlier analysis, the pupil does not suspend his own meanings and search out those of the teacher, and so he does not hear the teacher's final question as calling for a conforming reply. Both have set aside, for the moment, their normal classroom rules, and each allows the other to 'own' his particular body of facts and ideas.

This was an unusual exchange. We might have called it a side-sequence, except that in discussing the incident afterwards the teacher referred to his deliberate encouragement of the discussion because of the boys' involvement in it, and because it was the first time he had elicited more than monosyllabic responses from the more active pupil. In the context in which he was working, this teacher had the freedom to allow this incident without interfering with the work of others. But there were some examples of this change in learning role within the official curriculum, especially in the second year. These pupils were discussing with the teacher what they had learned about the Netsilik Eskimos:

7.14   T: Well, what about you, Yvonne?
         P: Think of the Eskimos?
         T: Yeah, think about the way they live — you know, what sort of things have struck you as you've looked at the films or thought about the way in which they live. ((Pause.))
         P: They have a thing about sons and daughters.
         T: Well, go on, what thing about sons and daughters?
         P: Well, if they're daughters, they feel they can't provide for her.
         T: Yeah.
         P: ((Very positively)) Sir, that's not *right*.
         T: Why?
         P: I don't know.
         T: When you say . . .
         P: It's their child and they *should* care for it.

Since these pupils have completed that part of their course, they too know some of the facts about the Eskimo way of life. Yvonne is not concerned to learn more facts, but to use what she knows already to form her own ideas. The teacher's question, 'What do you think about the Eskimos?', is a genuinely open question. He is not concerned with sharing his own interpretation, but with drawing out that of the pupil.

Opportunities for this sort of discussion were still rare, and resource-based learning has no monopoly of it. Indeed, as we have presented it here, it may be outside the conventional framework of such learning. In their planning for the following year's work, it was an activity which these Humanities teachers hoped would increase with the provision of more occasions for discussion where pupils could explore and use knowledge acquired in other, more teacher-controlled sections of the curriculum. As Barnes has argued, such opportunities are necessary if school knowledge is not to remain separated and remote from the everyday world — opportunities for pupils to integrate it with their commonsense knowledge.(20) Yvonne was taking an early, rather tentative, step on the road.

Chapter 7: Notes and References

1 Bernstein (1971), 'On the Classification and Framing of Educational Knowledge', in Young (ed.), *Knowledge and Control*.

2 Hammersley (1976), 'The Mobilization of Pupil Attention, in Hammersley and Woods (eds), *The Process of Schooling*.

3 This, of course, is the position taken by Flanders (1970), *Analysing Teaching Behaviour*.

4 This variable pattern has been documented by researchers from such widely diverse positions as Flanders (1970), op. cit., and Sinclair and Coulthard (1975), *Towards an Analysis of Discourse*.

5 Torode (1977), 'Interrupting Inter-subjectivity', in Woods and Hammersley (eds), *School Experience*.

6 As they were in the lesson described by Hammersley (1977), in Woods and Hammersley, op. cit.

7 There is an analogy here with Silverman and Jones's description of 'Interview Talk', Silverman and Jones (1976), *Organizational Work; the Language of Grading, the Grading of Language*.

8 This is a very obvious example of what Cicourel (1973), *Cognitive Sociology*, describes as a 'retrospective-prospective sense of occurrence'.

9 Stubbs (1976), in Stubbs and Delamont (eds), *Explorations in Classroom Observation*, argues that metastatements are the main means by which teachers control classroom events.

10 The idea that lessons can be divided up into different sections or sub-phases where different rules will apply has been illustrated both by Hargreaves, Hestor and Mellor (1975), *Deviance in Classrooms* and by Sinclair and Coulthard (1975), op. cit. Hargreaves *et al.* describe five different phases: entry, settling down, the lesson proper, clearing up, and exit. What we are describing here may be considered sub-phases within the lesson proper. They are akin to what Sinclair and Coulthard call 'transactions'.

11 These metastatements are what Sinclair and Coulthard (1975), op. cit., call focusing moves — they come at the beginning of a new 'transaction'. Hargreaves, Hestor and Mellor (1975), op. cit., describe them as 'task indicators' — part of the 'switch-signal' indicating which new situational rules are appropriate.

12 Walker and Adelman (1972), *Towards a Sociography of Classrooms*.

13 'Side-sequences' within therapy sessions are described by Turner (1972), 'Some Formal Properties of Therapy Talk', in Sudnow (ed.), *Studies in Social Interaction*.

14 A similar point is made by Walker and Adelman (1972), op. cit., who note how in this type of classroom the pupil is able to become much more of an individual to the teacher than in a formal class where only a few pupils, such as the 'court jester', stand out from the crowd. Because teachers and pupils work together, each apprehends the other as a unique individual — they develop a 'consociate' as opposed to a 'contemporary' relationship.

15 A comment made by Keddie (1971), on the Humanities lessons she observed; Keddie, 'Classroom Knowledge', in Young (ed.), op. cit.

16 Bernstein (1977), *Class, Codes and Control*, vol. 3, chapters 4 and 5. We

referred in Chapter 4 to examples of 'integrated' science where these conditions were *not* met.

17   All the quotations in these pages are taken from a tape-recorded discussion involving the writers and all five members of the Humanities team. Some of the proposed changes they refer to have in fact been carried out in 1977–8. There have been more occasions for class teaching, and more discussions involving groups of children. Of greater significance, much of the first-year course which we saw being taught has now been dropped. MACOS is introduced in the Easter term of the *first* year, and then extended in the second year by new work, devised by the team, on how and why human communities change. The new work begins with the local community, using extensive photographic material showing changes over the last century, and then moves outwards to other cases of material and cultural adaptation.

18   Bernstein (1977), op. cit., p. 84.
19   Bernstein (1977), op. cit., p. 101.
20   Barnes (1976), *From Communication to Curriculum*.

Chapter 8

Conclusion: Authority in Classroom Interaction

It is dangerously easy for researchers, whatever their methodological persuasion, to present their accounts as the best possible interpretation of events, inferior versions having been discarded along the way. But the inseparability of theory and data, on which we have insisted throughout this book, makes it impossible for us suddenly to offer a final or complete account of the teaching we observed. Many other 'realities' might have been reported, and we have to be on guard against jumping to conclusions without noticing 'the indefinite family of alternative possible readings'.(1) We certainly do not regard the evidence in Chapters 5–7 as proving a case. Even long stretches of transcript provide only the appearance of proof, because the relevant facts both exemplify *and are the basis of* the particular interpretation being offered. In other words, examples presented as evidence of various patterns of interaction cannot be interpreted without assuming the existence of those patterns.(2)

In the context of what we argued earlier about different research perspectives generating their own facts, this is an appropriately cautious beginning to our final chapter. But caution can be excessive. It might be suggested that we should have learned to live with these worries by now, and be ready to offer what is promised in the heading 'Conclusion'. What then have we learned from our investigation of classroom talk, and what generalizations do we feel justified in drawing from it?

The research outlined in Chapter 2 documented, in very different ways, a model of transmission teaching which is often modified but rarely transformed. Differences in the surface style of individual teachers seem to leave unaltered a basic structure of centrally controlled interaction and centrally managed meanings. It is this structure which makes classrooms so distinctive as settings for talk, and which has attracted researchers looking for evidence of it 'in the text' even when they strongly disapprove of the very characteristics on which their analysis depends. Most of these characteristics will certainly appear obvious to teachers accustomed to traditional classrooms. But some of them were also apparent in the untraditional classrooms which we observed. As a result of the emphasis on resource-based learning, these teachers have drawn away from giving performances in front of an audience towards more individualized diagnosis and treatment of learning difficulties. What this move has not done is to significantly reduce the teachers' control over the meanings being transmitted. This conclusion will be elaborated by recalling some of the main themes of the preceding three chapters. We do so in the present tense because it expresses 'the perspective of exploration'; the past tense is 'the perspective of confirmation', which is certainly more than we would claim.(3)

In much of what they do managerially, teachers assume and trade on pupils' ability and willingness to fill in the appropriate background meanings to what is actually said. Especially when they themselves initiate the interaction, they usually assume that these background meanings are the same as their own and that they can proceed on the basis of 'shared unspoken understandings of critical features of the context'.(4) The deepest level of common knowledge is about the 'proper' relationship of teacher and pupil, because without this the task of establishing procedural competence is difficult, and the main business of instruction cannot begin. But when it comes to the curriculum, teachers assume that meanings will not be shared until they have been taught. Pupils assume a complementary ignorance, suspending their own knowledge until they have located the teacher's frame of reference and can begin to move towards it. We have suggested that this movement can be achieved more successfully if the teacher is largely freed for large numbers of problem-solving encounters. But we should always remember *whose* problems are being solved. Teachers construct problems they can handle within their own frame of reference out of their pupils' much less specific difficulties. For much of the time, therefore, they are answering their own problems. It is still the pupils' sense and acceptance of the teacher's authority which provide the main basis for assigning instructional meanings. The process of control has been altered, but it has not been relaxed.

Now in suggesting that the teaching we observed differed much less from the transmission model than might have appeared on the surface, we must make it clear what kind of conclusion this is. We will begin with what it is *not*.

We do not see our work as a 'critical-case' study from which conclusions can be drawn about the typical features of resource-based learning.(5) Even in the guise of a case study with no strong claim to being representative, we do not see our findings as bringing news. That educational innovations often appear similar in consequence and even practice to the methods which they are intended to replace has long been recognized, not least by teachers themselves. 'Between appearance and reality falls the shadow.' Innovations may be subverted by the lack of necessary technical and organizational support; by the residual conservatism of teachers; by the incorrigible selective function of schools; and by the impossibility of escaping the forms of social relationship required by capitalist society. All these explanations of the failure radically to redefine classroom practice have appeared in recent research.(6) Yet unlike writers such as Sharp and Green, in their 'exposure' of progressive primary education, we do not see the teachers we observed as *unwittingly constrained*' in what they do by their failure to appreciate 'how the effects of a complex stratified society penetrate the school' in ways which 'belie both their moral commitments and the causes they appear to have adopted and profess'.(7) Our discussions with the Humanities team suggested that they were well aware of the limitations of what they were doing, and of the limits within which they worked. As we emphasized earlier, resource-based learning is not seen by them as a synonym for open or 'discovery' learning. They were aware of the external pressures for results (especially on a school known to be innovative); of the *relative* insulation of the Lower School from these pressures; of the temptations to revert to more traditional teaching in preparation for public examinations; and of more general tensions within the Centre over the apparently competing claims of autonomous learning and standards of excellence. As has often been argued, there are deep internal contradictions in resource-based learning — contradictions between the aims of an ideology devoted to personal development in a democratic setting, and the need to recognize the integrative functions of schooling where pupils must learn certain things and acquire basic skills.(8) Such contradictions in the present context are neatly illustrated in the booklet sent out to parents of new pupils, from which we quoted in Chapter 4; pupils learn to 'take more responsibility for their own work and progress' with the guidance of the teacher and within 'a carefully constructed programme of work'.

In view of these contradictions, it seems useful to see the teaching we observed as a coping strategy — a way of working developed to reconcile the difficult problems of maintaining order, communicating information, and providing at least some degree of pupil autonomy.(9) By planning the curriculum in detail, and by providing quantities of core and supplementary material, the teachers give themselves room to concentrate on the basic skills of reading and comprehension with slow learners and to deal with the difficulties of individual pupils, while allowing pupils generally at least some control over their activities. As a coping strategy, this approach to learning is highly institutionalized in the school. Although there is an extraordinary commitment to devising and revising clearly structured and imaginative curriculum materials, the large resources devoted to reprographic work throughout the Centre bring heavy constraints to produce *something*, and new members of teaching teams are quickly socialized into this way of working. It is a way which both reflects and reinforces the prescription of what knowledge is to be transmitted, and such opportunities as we have described for pupils to define their own problems (and the knowledge relevant to their solution) were excursions from the mainstream of the curriculum. More extensive and persistent departures from it would require a considerable restructuring of prevailing teaching strategies. Pupils' control over their own learning was therefore exercised within firm limits, and it was largely control over the pacing rather than the content of their work.

Although we earlier disclaimed for our research any justification by substantive results, our analysis of the teaching we observed might still seem to be identifying the typical structure of such teaching. But it is not our intention to prove the essential similarity of old and new methods of teaching; rather, we hope to demonstrate a way of recognizing similarities *when they occur*. There *were* considerable differences between the classrooms we observed, and classrooms where a central communication system makes the teacher's authority pervasively obvious because it is so publicly announced, tested, and reinforced. But the differences were less in the degree of teacher control than in the methods by which it was accomplished. If our research has been exploratory, and not at all concerned with the verifying of propositions, then what has been explored is a particular way of making sense of classroom interaction in very diverse contexts. We will elaborate this argument by taking up and extending the notion of *authority-talk* which was briefly introduced in Chapter 5 and extensively illustrated in the two chapters which followed. It is a notion which makes it possible to recognize a similar basic structure in talk in apparently very different contexts. As we argue in the rest of this chapter, it also makes it possible to show *how* this structure is produced and reproduced.

It is sometimes observed that teachers are 'underpowered' for the control which they are expected to maintain.(11) They have few frightening sanctions in their armoury, few sanctions of any kind which do not involve considerable inconvenience to themselves, and they suffer from the close proximity of those they have to keep in order because familiarity so often diminishes respect. They therefore have to work hard to maintain the appearance of being in charge, presenting various formal and informal rules as being facts of classroom life in the hope that these facts will only rarely be disputed. But accounts of despotism perilously preserved may be too preoccupied with the more dramatic aspects of control and conflict. There is no doubt that teachers *are* underpowered when the natural order breaks down. There is no doubt either that power is the ultimate basis of their authority, and that the existence or threat of sanctions underlies softer forms of social control. But we must ask how the teacher's authority is manifested and reproduced in the *routine* patterns of classroom talk.

We referred in Chapter 5 to the traditional sociological distinction between power and authority. Power implies a personal dominance, reality being defined for others whether they like it or not. Authority implies some measure of agreement, a recognition by those acceding to it of the legitimacy of the control being exercised over them.(12) In practice, this distinction is rarely clear, though where special rights are seen as the legitimate product of a status relationship, the power basis of that relationship may well be concealed. What Bernstein has called *positional* control may depend on an overt display of power in the form of commands backed by threats. But it more commonly derives from the authority inherent in the social relationship, an authority which normally makes it unnecessary either to threaten or to justify explicitly the required behaviour. The right to make the relevant decisions 'is invested in the member's formal status', little discretion is allowed to those being controlled, and 'any border disputes are settled by the relative power inhering in the respective statuses'.(13) Despite its abstract form, this description seems closely applicable to classrooms.(14) In Bernstein's terms, teacher—pupil relationships involve 'consistent and recognized forms of interaction', and the teacher normally controls 'the selection, organization and pacing of the knowledge transmitted and received'. At least in the area of instruction, there is only limited need and scope for negotiation. That phrase 'at least' must be emphasized. In the areas traditionally referred to as classroom management and classroom discipline, pupils have considerable power to negotiate and renegotiate a working consensus, both individually and collectively, and we are aware that by concentrating on the teacher's control of instructional meanings we are likely to make his authority seem too easily maintained and too easily granted.(15) But in the main business of the classroom, that of transmitting knowledge, classroom talk only makes sense as 'the working-out of a power relation', as 'the recognizable attempt of one party to grade the talk of the other'.(16)

That reference to the grading of talk is taken from a study of formal interviews, occasions which are 'the very antithesis of dialogue' because one participant has the right to elicit and assess the talk of the other. The interviewee's words are treated as evidence of some relevant qualities (of ability, reliability, social skills, and so on), and the interviewer orders his questions so as to uncover these patterns. The whole encounter is managed so as to do so effectively, and he has the right to define what has been uncovered. Now analogies are always dangerous, and we are not suggesting that teaching can be described as some kind of collective interview. The parallel we wish to draw relates not to the detailed organization of the talk, but to its general readability in terms of the hierarchical relationship of the speakers. If classroom talk can be read as evidence of what is obvious *to the participants*, then some notion of hierarchy seems to provide the most obvious context for it. What pupils say is certainly searched for evidence that they have entered, or are willing to enter, the teacher's frame of reference, and this searching is carried out by someone who has 'the right to know'. But this is one aspect of a persistent recourse to the teacher's authority as the taken-for-granted foundation on which teachers and pupils 'accomplish comprehensible talk and action'.(17) Both 'sides' *use* their structural relationship as a basis for expressing and assigning meanings, and in doing so they reconstitute that relationship.

An obvious example of authority-talk occurs when a pupil is simply told what to do without being given any explicit reason or justification. Some of the extracts we quoted earlier contain statements of what 'has to be done' which admit no possibility of alternative courses of action; for example, 'I should only have to ask you once to be quiet, and then everybody should be hushed straightaway'. Such an order can only be disregarded by challenging the whole basis of the relationship, in which case sanctions are likely to be employed, threatened, or implied. But teachers usually act on, and work out, their authority less obtrusively than this, and as long as their official definitions of the situation are not overtly contradicted, they can assume that these definitions are shared. This point can be restated so as to emphasize how the authority which underlies the interaction is constituted through its use. Teachers *have* authority in so far as pupils address them, and respond to them, as though they are indeed 'in charge'. We have described many of the forms which such acts of recognition regularly take. Pupils listen when required to do so, bid properly for the right to speak themselves, work without undue chatter, and seek the teacher's help when they 'can't get on'. Above all, they express in their talk a willingness to set their own knowledge aside as irrelevant, or as irrelevant until formulated in new ways, and to see as problems what had not seemed problematic to them before. Each and every encounter of this kind both reflects *and reconstitutes* the teacher's authority.

We saw in Chapter 5 how teachers relied on their pupils' basic knowledge of what classrooms were like to provide a framework within which various procedural details could be elaborated. We also argued that the separation of surface from base (or of procedural details from relationship knowledge) was merely an analytical convenience. As the teacher announced and elaborated detailed rules of procedure, he was also announcing and confirming his right to make such decisions. If such talk can be read as evidence of how the participants see their relationship, it is also an essential part *of* that relationship. The circularity we referred to as an inescapable dilemma in reporting research — that interaction which is interpreted as evidence of some underlying pattern is simultaneously taken as evidence of that pattern — is the foundation of all forms of social life. The background knowledge on which participants rely to make sense of their interaction is rarely made explicit; because it is taken for granted this is normally unnecessary. It is nevertheless being constantly demonstrated and confirmed in the course of interaction. This is the circularity so heavily emphasized in Bernstein's writing, where social structure is described as constraining what can properly be said (and meant) *and* as being announced and confirmed through the speech which is so constrained. It has also been emphasized in interpretive sociolinguistics, where social roles and identities are not seen as factors external to the interaction but as being signalled in the act of speaking, and where the context within which speech is interpreted is seen as being created through the speech which it supports. In these approaches, it is impossible to separate a structural from an interactionist perspective. We suggest that they also blur the equally venerable distinction between macro- and micro-level analysis.

We have attempted, then, to identify a basic structure in classroom interaction which represents for the participants both a constraint and a resource, and which is reconstituted as it is put to use. Its distinctive features are derived from the authority of the teacher to manage what is said and meant. Because the location of that authority has been taken no further than the immediate institutional context, our account is vulnerable to the criticism of being 'irredeemably conservative' for its failure to consider wider influences.(18) Now we entirely accept the argument that classroom research should attempt to show both the immediate flow of teacher–pupil interaction and 'some of the more or less subtle ways in which wider social structural "forces" impinge' upon it(19), and that it is futile to do one *or* the other in the hope that quite separate forms of analysis can be somehow added up to give the total picture.(20) Thus Bowles and Gintis can be criticized because they simply infer the kinds of social relationship which must exist in the schools of capitalist society to reproduce the appropriate social hierarchies, while the other side of the macro–micro division of sociological labour, ethnographic studies of classroom life sometimes ignore the opportunities which are objectively available and the constraints which are objectively in force. The best sociology has always tried to show on the one hand how 'all talk of structures and functions must refer in the end to people doing things together', and on the other how interaction must be located within its 'concentric milieux' so as to identify those personal troubles which are also public issues.(21) But this formidable task is not necessarily carried out by moving systematically from one level of analysis to another. We might indeed try to locate the teaching we observed by moving out from the classroom to (for example) the organizational resources which supported it; to the shortages of resources which constrained it; to the conflicting expectations of colleagues, parents, and LEA officials; to the long shadow of marketable educational qualifications; and then to the even longer shadow thrown by gross inequalities in society at large. It seems to us extremely difficult to show how such forces get into classroom interaction by making some kind of remorselessly systematic analysis. It is certainly difficult to show relationships between the macroscopic orderings of society and teachers' perceptions of reality without recourse to the old stand-by of 'false consciousness'.(22) The approach which we have tried to follow avoids the traditional macro–micro distinction by showing both 'the constitution of actors by society' *and* 'the production and reproduction of society by actors'.(23)

It *is* essential to observe people 'doing things together' to avoid the crude determinism of explaining their behaviour by reference to external forces which cannot themselves be observed. But the recognition that social life is 'always and everywhere a skilled accomplishment of its members' should be accompanied by the recognition that it is not accomplished 'merely under conditions of their own choosing'. Reading Anthony Giddens's account of what he calls structuration, some months after our own work was completed, we recognized a more abstract version of the process which we had been concerned with ourselves. The concept is an attempt to 'complement the idea of the production of social life with that of the social reproduction of structures'. It refers to the process by which 'social structures are both constituted by human agency and yet at the same time are the very medium of this constitution'.(24) These structures are both inferred from social interaction and a medium through which interaction in that form is possible. Our analysis of classroom interaction requires little translation to fit this framework. It is through recourse to their sense of a structural relationship that teachers and pupils repeatedly reconstitute that structure, which is both the basis *for* their interaction *and* a product of it.

Even exploratory studies which disclaim any verifying of new facts may bring insights by presenting the familiar in a different light. By making explicit what is normally taken for granted, they may help teachers, 'should they so wish, no longer to take it for granted'.(25) Such explorations of the 'obvious' can then be a preliminary to change on the grounds — so optimistically expressed by Waller — that 'whatever contributes to the understanding of human life must one day contribute to its reconstruction'. But even if we had intended to end with a prescription for reconstructing classroom life, we recognize that changing teachers' consciousness would be a necessary but insufficient basis for it. We do believe, however, that some kinds of classroom research (including, of course, our own) have made it possible to see more clearly the authoritative nature of teacher–pupil relationships. There are severe functional restrictions on what pupils can say because what they can mean is normally bounded by what the teacher considers to be relevant, appropriate, and correct. As we suggested earlier, it is tempting to apply Halliday's more general comment to classrooms, and to see them as contexts where 'meaning potential' is subject to highly asymmetrical processes of definition, and where the semantic options available to pupils 'are rather closely specifiable'. Clearly implicit in such a comment is our view that pupils are too *consistently* treated as consumers of knowledge in a context where they have 'little status and few rights'.(26) If they are sometimes to engage in recoding the knowledge offered to them, or even in constructing meanings in a context in which what they say is responded to rather than being assessed, then the authority of the teacher as expert cannot consistently be the main basis for accomplishing comprehensible talk and action.(27) Even in contexts where they have greater control over the pacing of their work, pupils may still be learning that knowledge is what is known by those in authority, and the 'hierarchy between knowledge-producers, transmitters and consumers' may remain intact.(28) But our concern here is with diagnosis, not prescription. Our conclusion is not a set of facts, but a way of exploring some of the structural conditions necessary for, and recognizable in, varieties of teaching. Close attention to the interpretative schemes which teachers and pupils seem to be using to construct and assign meanings makes it possible to identify the extent to which different teaching strategies reflect and reproduce less hierarchical relationships, and less sharply differentiated boundaries between teachers' and pupils' knowledge.

Chapter 8: Notes and References

1   Torode (1976), 'Teachers' Talk and Classroom Discipline', in Stubbs and Delamont (eds), *Explorations in Classroom Observation*, p. 180.

2   This circularity is a basic problem in all social scientific research. It is well discussed in Wootton (1975), *Dilemmas of Discourse*, chapter 1 It is itself exemplified in Wieder (1974), 'Telling the Code', in Turner (ed.), *Ethnomethodology*. The code of conduct seen as governing the behaviour of prisoners and staff is described by Wieder as 'a self-elaborating schema. Each newly encountered "piece" of talk was simultaneously rendered sensible by interpreting it in terms of the developing relevancies of the code and was, at the same time, more evidence of the existence of that code'. This was how the code worked for him as observer, *and* for those whose behaviour he was observing.

3   Stebbins (1975), *Teachers and Meaning*, p. 50.

4   Bernstein (1973), *Class, Codes and Control*, vol. 1, p. 32.

5   For reasons which we outline later in the chapter, we doubt if the teaching we observed was typical even of the Abraham Moss Centre.

6   For example, and in substantive order: Hamilton (1973), 'The Integration of Knowledge: Practice and Problems', *J. Curr. Studies* 5; Stenhouse (1973), 'The Humanities Project', in Butcher and Pont (eds), *Educational Research in Britain* 3; Sharp and Green (1975), *Education and Social Control*; Bowles and Gintis (1976), *Schooling in Capitalist America*.

7   Sharp and Green (1975), op. cit., pp. vii–viii. We have therefore not been inhibited from naming the teachers we observed, as they were, because identifying the social-structural constraints within which they work might appear to impugn their motives.

8   These contradictions are discussed at length in Hargreaves, A. (1977), 'Progressivism and Pupil Autonomy', *Sociol. Rev.* 25.3.

9   The idea of a coping strategy is elaborated by Hargreaves, A. (1977), op. cit.

10 There have been moves by the Humanities team in the present academic year to open out parts of the course, and to respond to pupils' interests. For example, a unit on the impact of the slave trade on West African communities was devised because of interest in the television showing of *Roots*. Other changes made since our regular visits to the school are outlined in Chapter 7, note 17.

11 Musgrove (1971), *Patterns of Power and Authority in English Education*, pp. 2–3, 30–8, offers a lively example of this view.

12 Gerth and Mills (1970), *From Max Weber*.

13 Bernstein (1973), op. cit., pp. 176–9. In an earlier discussion of what he later called person-oriented families, Bernstein recognized that even where more overtly rational methods of control were employed, 'power in the end is still the ultimate basis of authority' (1973, p. 66).

14 Bernstein's description, of course, is of parental control of children. Its relevance to teachers' control of pupils is argued by Cooper (1976), *Bernstein's Codes: A Classroom Study*.

15 The power of pupils in establishing this consensus is well described in Hargreaves (1972), *Interpersonal Relations and Education*, chapter 6.

16 Silverman and Jones (1976), *Organizational Work*, p. 22.
17 Silverman and Jones (1976), op. cit., p. 9.
18 This point is made by Hamilton and Delamont (1974), 'Classroom Research: A Cautionary Tale', *Res. in Educ.* 11, and echoed in Delamont (1976), *Interaction in the Classroom*.
19 Sharp and Green (1975), op. cit., p. vii.
20 That an 'exciting sociological account' should reveal 'the relationships between structural features and interactional practices in a context of change' is strongly argued in Bernstein (1977), *Class, Codes and Control*, vol.3, chapter 7. The normal practice of concentrating on structure *or* interaction is well described in the introduction to Karabel and Halsey (eds) (1977), *Knowledge and Ideology in Education*.
21 These complementary prescriptions are taken from Becker (1970), *Sociological Work*, p. v; and Mills (1970), *The Sociological Imagination*, pp. 19−21.
22 For some valiant attempts to show *how* 'the values embodied in current conceptions of curricular knowledge and the styles of pedagogy and assessment adopted by teachers . . . help to sustain existing social hierarchies', see Whitty and Young (eds) (1976), *Explorations in the Politics of School Knowledge*, and Young and Whitty (eds) (1977), *Society, State and Schooling*. The papers by Whitty in these books are particularly interesting. See also Hammersley (1977), 'School Learning: The Cultural Resources Required by Pupils to Answer a Teacher's Question', in Woods and Hammersley (eds), *School Experience*.
23 Giddens (1976), *New Rules of Sociological Method*, p. 22.
24 Giddens (1976), op. cit., pp. 121−2. Reading Giddens's book, we felt rather as Smith and Geoffrey did when the label 'microethnography of a classroom' was suggested as a description of their work — that structuration was what we had been concerned with all along, and that it was 'both high-sounding and important'. In fact, something like this concept is now very much in the air in sociology. For example, Bourdieu's work has been centrally concerned with social and cultural reproduction through the 'structuring of structure', and his perspective is applied directly (if abstrusely) to the authority of the teacher in Bourdieu and Passeron, *Reproduction in Education, Society and Culture*, pp. 4−29.
25 This is the justification offered by Hargreaves and his colleagues for their study of *Deviance in Classrooms*.
26 Bernstein (1977), op. cit., chapter 5.
27 For an excellent analysis of the classroom conditions necessary to support exploratory learning, see Barnes (1976), *From Communication to Curriculum*, and Barnes and Todd (1977), *Communication and Learning in Small Groups*.
28 Whitty (1976), 'Studying Society: For Social Change or Social Control', in Whitty and Young (eds), op. cit., p. 39; and Hammersley (1977), op. cit., p. 83.

Bibliography

Ackerman, J. (1972), *Operant-Conditioning Techniques for the Classroom Teacher* (Scott, Foresman).

Adams, R. (1971), 'A Sociological Approach to Classroom Research', in I. Westbury and A. Bellack (eds), *Research into Classroom Processes* (Teachers' College Press).

Adams, R. and Biddle, B. (1970), *Realities of Teaching: Explorations with Videotape* (Holt, Rinehart and Winston).

Amidon, E. and Hough, J. (eds) (1967), *Interaction Analysis: Theory and Research* (Addison-Wesley).

Amidon, E. and Hunter, E. (1967), *Improving Teaching: The Analysis of Verbal Interaction* (Holt, Rinehart and Winston).

Anderson, H. (1939), 'The Measurement of Dominative and Socially Integrative Behaviour in Teachers' Contacts with Children', *Child Development* 10, pp. 73–89; also in Amidon and Hough (1967), op. cit.

Andreski, S. (1974), *Social Science as Sorcery* (Penguin Books).

Ashby, M. C. and Coulthard, R. M. (1976) 'A Linguistic Analysis of Doctor–Patient Interviews' in M. Wadsworth and D. Robinson (eds), *Studies in Everyday Medical Life* (Martin Robertson).

Barnes, D. (1969), 'Language in the Secondary Classroom', in D. Barnes, J. Britton and H. Rosen, *Language, the Learner and the School* (Penguin Books).

——— (1976), *From Communication to Curriculum* (Penguin Books).

Barnes, D. and Shemilt, D. (1974), 'Transmission and Interpretation', *Educational Review* 26, pp. 213–28.

Barnes, D. and Todd, F. (1977), *Communication and Learning in Small Groups* (Routledge and Kegan Paul).

Bealing, D. (1973), 'Issues in Classroom Observational Research', *Research in Education* 9, pp. 70–82.

Becker, H. (1970), *Sociological Work: Method and Substance* (Allen Lane, the Penguin Press).

Bellack, A., Kliebard, H., Hyman, R., and Smith, F. (1966), *The Language of the Classroom* (Teachers' College Press).

Bernstein, B. (1971), 'On the Classification and Framing of Educational Knowledge', in M. Young (ed), *Knowledge and Control: New Directions in the Sociology of Education* (Collier-Macmillan).

——— (1973), *Class, Codes and Control: Vol. 1 – Theoretical Studies towards a Sociology of Language* (Paladin Books: first published by Routledge and Kegan Paul, 1971).

——— (1977), *Class, Codes and Control: Vol. 3 – Towards a Theory of Educational Transmissions* (2nd. Edition) (Routledge and Kegan Paul).

Biddle, B. (1967), 'Methods and Concepts in Classroom Research', *Review of Educational Research* 37, pp. 337–57.

Blom, J-P and Gumperz, J. (1972), 'Social Meaning in Linguistic Structures', in J. Gumperz and D. Hymes (eds), *Directions in Sociolinguistics: The Ethnography of Communication* (Holt, Rinehart and Winston).

Bourdieu, P and Passeron, J-C. (1977), *Reproduction in Education, Society and Culture* (Sage).

Bowles, S. and Gintis, H. (1976), *Schooling in Capitalist America* (Routledge and Kegan Paul).

Bruner, J. (1966), *Towards a Theory of Instruction* (Harvard University Press).

Bullock, A. (Chairman) (1975), *A Language for Life* (The Bullock Report) (Department of Education and Science: H.M.S.O.).

Cazden, C., John, V. and Hymes, D. (eds) (1972), *The Functions of Language in the Classroom* (Teachers' College Press).

Chanan, G. and Delamont, S. (eds) (1975), *Frontiers of Classroom Research* (National Foundation for Educational Research).

Cicourel, A. (1973), *Cognitive Sociology* (Penguin Books).

——— (1974), 'Some Basic Theoretical Issues in the Assessment of the Child's Performance in Testing and Classroom Settings', in A. Cicourel *et al.*, *Language Use and School Performance* (Academic Press).

Cole, M., Gay, J. *et al* (1971), *The Cultural Context of Learning and Thinking* (Methuen).

Cooper, B. (1976), *Bernstein's Codes: a Classroom Study* (University of Sussex Education Area: Occasional Paper, no. 6).

Delamont, S. (1976a), *Interaction in the Classroom* (Methuen).

——— (1976b), 'Beyond Flanders' Fields: The Relationship of Subject-Matter and Individuality to Classroom Style', in M. Stubbs and S. Delamont (eds), *Explorations in Classroom Observation* (Wiley).

Dumont, R. (1972), 'Learning English and How to Be Silent: Studies in Sioux and Cherokee Classrooms' in C. Cazden *et al.* (eds), op. cit.

Edwards, A. (1976), *Language in Culture and Class: The Sociology of Language and Education* (Heinemann Educational Books).

——— (1978), 'The Language of History and the Communication of Historical Knowledge', in A. Dickinson and P. Lee (eds), *History Teaching and Historical Understanding* (Heinemann Educational Books).

Eggleston, J., Galton, M. and Jones, M. (1975), *A Science-Teaching Observation Schedule* (Science Research Studies: Macmillan).

——— (1976), *Processes and Products of Science Teaching* (Science Research Studies: Macmillan).

Ervin-Tripp, S. (1972), 'Sociolinguistic Rules of Address', in J. Pride and J. Holmes (eds), *Sociolinguistics* (Penguin Books).

Firth, J. (1957), *Papers in Linguistics 1934–51* (Oxford University Press).

Fishman, J. and Salmon, E. (1972), 'What has the Sociology of Language to say to the Teacher?', in C. Cazden *et al.* (eds), op. cit.

Flanders, N. (1967), 'Interaction Models of Critical Teaching Behaviour', in E. Amidon and J. Hough (eds), op. cit.

——— (1970), *Analysing Teacher Behaviour* (Addison-Wesley).

Frender, R. and Lambert, W. (1972), 'Speech Style and Scholastic Success', in

R. Shuy (ed), *Sociolinguistics: Current Trends and Prospects* (Georgetown University Press).

Furlong, V. (1976), 'Interaction Sets in the Classroom: Towards a Study of Pupil Knowledge', in M. Stubbs and S. Delamont (eds), op. cit.

——— (1977), 'Anancy Goes to School', in P. Woods and M. Hammersley (eds), *School Experience* (Croom Helm).

Furlong, V. and Edwards, A. (1977), 'Language in Classroom Interaction: Theory and Data', *Educational Research* 19, pp. 122–8.

Gallagher, J. and Aschner, M. (1963), 'A Preliminary Report on Analyses of Classroom Inter-action', *Merrill-Palmer Quarterly* 9, pp. 183–94.

Gallagher, J., Nuthall, G. and Rosenshine, B. (1970), *Classroom Observation* (American Educational Research Association Monograph: Rand McNally).

Gannaway, H. (1976), 'Making Sense of School', in Stubbs and Delamont (eds), op. cit.

Garfinkel, H. (1964), 'Studies in the Routine Grounds of Everyday Activities', *Social Problems* 11, pp. 225–50.

——— (1967), *Studies in Ethnomethodology* (Prentice-Hall).

Gerth, H. and Mills, C. (eds) (1970), *From Max Weber: Essays in Sociology* (Routledge and Kegan Paul.

Getzels, J. (1974), 'Images of the Classroom and Visions of the Learner', *School Review* 82, pp. 527–40.

Giddens, A. (1976), *New Rules of Sociological Method: A Positive Critique of Interpretative Sociologies* (Hutchinson).

Goffman, E. (1963), *Behaviour in Public Places* (Collier-Macmillan).

Gumperz, J. (1971), *Language in Social Groups* (Stanford University Press).

Gumperz, J. and Herasimchuk, E. (1972), 'The Conversational Analysis of Social Meaning: A Study of Classroom Interaction', in R. Shuy (ed), *Sociolinguistics: Current Trends and Prospects* (Georgetown University Press).

Gumperz, J. and Hymes, D. (ed) (1972), *Directions in Sociolinguistics: The Ethnography of Communication* (Holt, Rinehart and Winston).

Hall, J. (1975), 'Forging Links with a Social System', *Education* 21 (February), pp. 202–3.

Halliday, M. (1973), *Explorations in the Functions of Language* (Arnold).

——— (1975), 'Talking One's Way in', in A. Davies (ed), *Problems of Language and Learning* (Heinemann Educational Books).

Hamilton, D. (1973), 'The Integration of Knowledge: Practice and Problems', *Journal of Curriculum Studies* 5, pp. 146–55.

——— (1975), 'Handling Innovation in the Classroom: Two Scottish Examples', in W. Reid and D. Walker (eds), *Case Studies in Curriculum Change* (Routledge and Kegan Paul).

Hamilton, D. and Delamont, S., 'Classroom Research: A Cautionary Tale', *Research in Education* 11, pp. 1–16.

Hammersley, M. (1974), 'The Organisation of Pupil Participation', *Sociological Review* 1, pp. 355–67.

——— (1976), 'The Mobilisation of Pupil Attention', in M. Hammersley and P. Woods (eds), op. cit.

——— (1977), 'School Learning: The Cultural Resources Required by Pupils to

Answer a Teacher's Question', in P. Woods and M. Hammersley (eds), op. cit.

Hammersley, M. and Woods, P. (eds) (1976), *The Process of Schooling: A Sociological Reader* (Routledge and Kegan Paul and Open University Press).

Hannan, A. (1975), 'The Problem of the Unmotivated Pupil in an Open School: A Participant-Observation Study', in Chanan and Delamont (eds), op. cit.

Hargreaves, A. (1977), 'Progressivism and Pupil Autonomy', *Sociological Review* 25, pp. 585—621.

Hargreaves, D. (1972), *Interpersonal Relations and Education* (Routledge and Kegan Paul).

Hargreaves, D., Hestor, S. and Mellor, F. (1975), *Deviance in Classrooms* (Routledge and Kegan Paul).

Herman, T. (1977), *Creating Learning Environments: The Behavioural Approach to Education* (Allyn and Bacon).

Hilsum, S. and Cane, B. (1971), *The Teacher's Day* (National Foundation for Educational Research).

Hoetker, J. and Ahlbrand, W. (1969), 'The Persistence of the Recitation', *American Educational Research Journal* 6, pp. 145—67.

Houston, S. (1970), 'A Re-Examination of Some Assumptions about the Language of Disadvantaged Children', *Child Development* 41, pp. 599—607.

Hunter, E. (1972), *Encounter in the Classroom: New Ways of Teaching* (Holt, Rinehart and Winston).

Hymes, D. (1972), 'On Communicative Competence', in J. Pride and J. Holmes (eds), *Sociolinguistics* (Penguin Books).

——— (1977), *Foundations in Sociolinguistics: An Ethnographic Approach* (Tavistock Publications).

Jackson, P. (1968), *Life in Classrooms* (Holt, Rinehart and Winston).

Jackson, P. and Lahaderue (1967), 'Inequalities of Teacher-Pupil Contacts', *Psychology in the Schools* 4, also in A. Morrison and D. McIntyre (eds) *The Social Psychology of Teaching*.

John, V. (1971), 'Language and Educability', in E. Leacock (ed), *The Culture of Poverty: A Critique* (Simon and Schuster).

Jones, R. (1968), *Fantasy and Feeling in Education* (University of London Press).

Karabel, J. and Halsey, A. (1977) (eds), *Power and Ideology in Education* (Oxford University Press).

Keddie, N. (1971), 'Classroom Knowledge', in M. Young (ed), *Knowledge and Control* (Collier-Macmillan).

Kliebard, H. (1966), 'Dimensions of Meaning in Classroom Discourse', *Journal of Teacher Education* 17, pp. 233—44.

Leiter, K. (1974), 'Ad Hocing in the Schools: A Study of Placement Practices in the Kindergartens of Two Schools', in Cicourel *et al.*, *Language Use and School Performance*; also (abridged) in Hammersley and Woods (eds), (1976), op. cit.

Martin, W. (1975), 'The Negotiated Order of Teachers in Team-Teaching Situations', *Sociology of Education* 48, pp. 202—22.

Massialas, B. and Zevin, J. (1967), *Creative Encounters in the Classrooms* (Wiley).

Meacham, M. and Wiesen, A. (1973), *Changing Classroom Behaviour: A Manual for Precision Teaching* (International Textbook Company).

Medley, D. and Mitzel, H. (1963), 'The Scientific Study of Teacher Behaviour', in A. Bellack (ed), *Theory and Research in Teaching* (Teachers' College Press).

Mehan, H. (1974), 'Accomplishing Classroom Lessons', in Cicourel *et al.*, *Language Use and School Behaviour* (Academic Press).

Mills, C. Wright (1970), *The Sociological Imagination* (Penguin Books).

Mishler, E. (1972), 'Implications of Teacher Strategies for Language and Cognition', in Cazden *et al.* (eds), op. cit.

Mitson, R. (1974), 'With Community in Mind', *Secondary Education* 4, pp. 108–10.

—— (1977), 'Resources not for Resources Sake', in Jennings (ed), *Management and Headship in the Secondary School* (Ward Lock).

Mitson, R. and Holder, M. (1974), 'Comprehensive Education within a Community Centre', *Forum* 16.3, pp. 88–91.

Musgrove, F. (1971), *Patterns of Power and Authority in English Education* (Methuen).

Nuthall, G. and Snook, I. (1973), 'Contemporary Models of Teaching', in R. Travers (ed), *Second Handbook of Research in Teaching* (Rand McNally).

Ober, R., Bentley, E. and Miller, E. (1971), *Systematic Observation of Teaching: An Interaction-Analysis Instructional Strategy Approach* (Prentice-Hall).

Philips, S. (1972), 'Participant-Structures and Communicative Competence: Warm Springs Children in Community and Classroom', in Cazden *et al.* (eds), op. cit.

Robinson, P. (1974), 'An Ethnography of Classrooms', in J. Eggleston (ed), *Contemporary Research in the Sociology of Education* (Methuen).

Rosenshine, B. and Furst, N. (1973), 'The Use of Direct Observation to Study Teaching', in R. Travers (ed), *Second Handbook of Research in Teaching* (Rand McNally).

Rutherford, R. (1976), 'Talking about Pop', in S. Rogers (ed), *They Don't Speak Our Language* (Arnold).

Sharp, R. and Green, A. (1975), *Education and Social Control: A Study in Progressive Primary Education* (Routledge and Kegan Paul).

Silverman, D. and Jones, J. (1976), *Organisational Talk: The Language of Grading and the Grading of Language* (Collier-Macmillan).

Simon, A. and Boyer, G. (eds) (1970), *Mirrors for Behaviour: An Anthology of Classroom Observation Instruments* (II) Research for Better Schools Inc.

Sinclair, J. and Coulthard, M. (1975), *Towards an Analysis of Discourse: The Language of Teachers and Pupils* (Oxford University Press).

Skinner, B. (1968), *The Technology of Teaching* (Appleton-Century-Crofts).

Smith, B., Meux, O. *et al.* (1970), *A Study of the Logic of Teaching* (University of Illinois Press).

Smith, L. and Geoffrey, W. (1968), *The Complexities of an Urban Classroom* (Holt, Rinehart and Winston).

Speier, M. (1973), *How to Observe Face-To-Face Communication: A Sociological Introduction* (Goodyear).

—— (1976), 'The Child as Conversationalist: Some Culture-Contact Features of Conversational Interactions between Adults and Children', in Hammersley and Woods (eds), op. cit.

Stebbins, R. (1973), 'Physical Context Influences on Behaviour: The Case of Classroom Disorderliness', *Environment and Behaviour* 5, pp. 291–314; also in Hammersley and Woods (eds) op. cit.

—— (1975), *Teachers and Meaning: Definitions of Classroom Situations* (Brill).

Stenhouse, L. (1969), 'Open-Minded Teaching', *New Society* 14, pp. 126–8.

—— (1973), 'The Humanities Project', in H. Butcher and H. Pont, (eds) *Educational Research in Britain – 3*.

Stubbs, M. (1976a), 'Keeping in Touch: Some Functions of Teacher-Talk', in Stubbs and Delamont (eds), op. cit.

—— (1976b), *Language, Schools and Classrooms* (Methuen).

Stubbs, M. and Delamont, S. (eds) (1976), *Explorations in Classroom Observation* (Wiley).

Sudnow, D. (1965), 'Normal Crimes: Sociological Features of the Penal Code in a Public Defender Office', *Social Problems* 12.

—— (ed), (1972), *Studies in Social Interaction* (Free Press).

Torode, B. (1976), 'Teachers' Talk and Classroom Discipline', in Stubbs and Delamont (eds), op. cit.

—— (1977), 'Interrupting Intersubjectivity', in Woods and Hammersley (eds), *School Experience* (Croom Helm).

Trudgill, P. (1975), *Accent, Dialect and the School* (Arnold).

Turner, R. (1970), 'Words, Utterances and Activities', in J. Douglas (ed), *Understanding Everyday Life* (Routledge and Kegan Paul).

—— (1972), 'Some Formal Properties of Therapy Talk', in Sudnow (ed) op. cit.

Walker, R. (1972), 'The Sociology of Education and Life in School Classrooms', *International Review of Education* 18, pp. 32–41.

Walker, R. and Adelman, C. (1972), *Towards a Sociography of Classrooms*, SSRC Report: Centre for Science Education, Chelsea College.

—— (1975a), 'Interaction Analysis in Informal Classrooms: A Critical Comment on the Flanders' System.' *British Journal of Educational Psychology* 45, pp. 73–6.

—— (1975b), *A Guide to Classroom Observation* (Methuen).

—— (1976), 'Strawberries', in Stubbs and Delamont (eds), op. cit.

Waller, W. (1965), *The Sociology of Teaching* (Wiley, first published 1932).

Wegman, R. (1976), 'Classroom Discipline: An Exercise in the Maintenance of Social Reality', *Sociology of Education* 49, pp. 71–9.

Weller, R. (1971), *Verbal Communication in Instructional Supervision* (Teachers' College Press).

Westbury, I. (1973), 'Conventional Classrooms, "Open" Classrooms, and the Technology of Teaching', *Journal of Curriculum Studies* 5, pp. 95–121.

Whitty, G. and Young, M. (eds) (1976), *Explorations in the Politics of School Knowledge* (Nafferton Books).

Whitty, G. (1977), 'Sociology and the Problem of Radical Educational Change', in Young and Whitty (eds), op. cit.

Wieder, L. (1974), 'Telling the Code', in R. Turner (ed), *Ethnomethodology* (Penguin Books).

Wight, J. (1976), 'Speech Acts: Thought Acts', *Educational Review* 28, pp. 168–79.

Woods, P. (1976a), 'Having a Laugh: An Antidote to Schooling', in Hammersley and Woods (eds), op. cit.

———— (1976b), 'Pupils' Views of School', *Educational Review* 28, pp. 126–137.

———— (1977), 'Teaching for Survival', in Woods and Hammersley (eds), op. cit.

Woods, P. and Hammersley, M. (eds) (1977), *School Experience* (Croom Helm).

Worrall, *et al.* (1970), *Teaching from Strength: An Introduction to Team Teaching* (Hamilton).

Wootton, A. (1975), *Dilemmas of Discourse: Controversies about the Sociological Interpretation of Language* (Allen and Unwin).

Wragg, E. (1974), *Teaching Teaching* (David and Charles).

———— (1975), 'The First Generation of British Interaction Studies', in Chanan and Delamont (eds), op. cit.

Young, M. and Whitty, G. (eds) (1977), *Society, State and Schooling* (Falmer Press).

Subject Index